THE BRAVERY EFFECT

"In *The Bravery Effect*, Jill Schulman offers a compelling parable that delves into the science of overcoming fear and embracing challenges. This book is a testament to the transformative power of bravery, providing practical strategies for personal growth and resilience. Through its engaging narrative, *The Bravery Effect* invites readers to step into the unknown, embracing discomfort as a catalyst for success and fulfillment. As someone who has dedicated his life to cultivating mental toughness and leadership, I think you will find this book a valuable resource for anyone seeking to unlock their full potential."

—MARK DIVINE, retired Navy SEAL commander, founder of SEALFIT and Unbeatable Mind, and *NYT* best-selling author

"*The Bravery Effect* is more than a story—it's a wake-up call. Alex's journey is your journey—whether you like it or not. As every Marine knows, you need to get comfortable being uncomfortable—the best things in life are found on the other side of hard. This book will challenge you, and if you let it, it will change you. I only wish I had read it 40 years ago."

—LT. GEN. ROBERT MILSTEAD, USMC (Ret.)

"How do we become braver versions of ourselves—at work and beyond? In *The Bravery Effect*, Jill Schulman brings the science of bravery to life through a riveting and relatable story. It's entertaining, wise, and practical—offering tools to elevate your success, impact, and potential. You'll be inspired to apply it to your own life—and likely pass it on to someone you care about. I was especially moved by the focus on brave relationships, a powerful and often overlooked key to growth."

—JANE DUTTON, professor of psychology and business administration, University of Michigan Ross School of Business

"History, science and psychology tell us that bravery is the key to a meaningful life and I'm thankful that Jill and *The Bravery Effect* show us how to be brave in spite of the fear and doubt that hold us back. This is the best and most impactful book on bravery I've ever read and I encourage you to start reading it today!"

—JON GORDON, best-selling author of *The Energy Bus* and *The One Truth*

"Unlock your inner courage and transform your life. In *The Bravery Effect*, author Jill Schulman masterfully blends the power of storytelling with the proven science of bravery to guide you on a transformative journey. Jill Schulman, with her background in the Marine Corps, corporate America, leadership development, and positive psychology, has created a book that is both insightful and deeply practical. *The Bravery Effect* promises to be the bridge that connects your desire for a bigger life with the scientific strategies to achieve it. Don't just weather the storms of life—learn to seek the winds of change and unlock the brave person within. Prepare to be inspired, challenged, and ultimately empowered to step into bravery and create a life without regret."

—DAN TOMASULO, PhD, academic director for Spirituality Mind Body Institute, Teachers College, Columbia University, and best-selling author of *Learned Hopefulness* and *The Positivity Effect*

"In *The Bravery Effect*, Jill Schulman reminds us that true satisfaction and growth come from embracing challenge. A gifted storyteller and experienced leader, she reveals the elements of bravery through the journey of an ordinary man adapting to life's trials. As a Marine, I recognize the truth in her message—courage is built, not born. This book will motivate you to escape the comfort trap and take bold ownership of your path. It's a powerful and highly readable call to action—and a road map to success."

—GENERAL JOSEPH F. DUNFORD, Jr., USMC (Ret.),
former chairman of the Joint Chiefs of Staff

"Inventive, provocative, and well-researched, *The Bravery Effect* maps the power of stepping outside your comfort zone to spark meaningful, sustainable growth—for yourself, your team, and your organization. A great story hits different than mere stats and studies, and Jill Schulman proves it by distilling decades of research and real-life experience into a compelling parable that sticks—and inspires."

—SHAWN ACHOR, *NYT* best-selling author of
The Happiness Advantage and *Big Potential*

"Reading *The Bravery Effect* was like lookig in a mirror. Jill Schulman's parable helped me recognize where I've been holding back—and gave me a clear roadmap to be braver. Her blend of Stoic wisdom and positive psychology, especially insights aligned with Dr. Martin Seligman's work, made the lessons feel both timeless and actionable. It reminded me that regret often comes from inaction—and that bravery begins in the mind. This isn't just a book for big decisions; it's a guide for anyone who leads, mentors, or wants to grow."

—JOHN REGISTER, CPAE Hall of Fame speaker, Paralympic
silver medalist, combat veteran, leadership speaker & coach

"Bravery is often misunderstood as something rare or reserved for heroic moments. In truth, it's a daily practice—and one of the most powerful pathways to self-actualization. In *The Bravery Effect*, Jill Schulman offers a thoughtful, science-backed story that's both practical and profound. If you're ready to grow into the person you're capable of becoming, this book is a meaningful place to start."

—SCOTT BARRY KAUFMAN, PhD,
humanistic psychologist and author of *Transcend*

"This is the book I wish someone had handed me years ago. It would have saved me a lot of unnecessary struggles. *The Bravery Effect* makes one truth very clear: Success lives on the other side of discomfort. Every business leader who wants a stronger team, a healthier culture, and a more courageous company should read this book. It's filled with powerful, life-changing ideas that will stay with you long after the last page."

—JOHN SPENCE, business and leadership expert

"Jill Schulman has written the parable we didn't know we needed—a smart, science-backed, and deeply human story that shows how everyday bravery is the secret ingredient to living a big, bold, regret-free life. As someone who has studied grit and goal setting for decades, I can say with confidence: *The Bravery Effect* will wake people up and change lives."

—CAROLINE ADAMS MILLER, author of global bestsellers
Creating Your Best Life, Getting Grit, and *Big Goals*

"Bravery fuels greatness, and *The Bravery Effect* is rocket fuel. It challenges your thinking, inspires action, and gives you a framework to build a braver life and business. The story format makes the principles relatable and brings them to life. The parable makes it personal. The science makes it powerful."

—CURTIS MORLEY, emotionologist and CEO of Counterfeit Emotions

"Not your typical self-help book, *The Bravery Effect* is a compelling, science-informed parable about learning to become braver. While the Bravery Sciences Institute doesn't exist—yet—Alex's journey and his notebook offer a powerful foundation for understanding how to take worthwhile risks. What would your own Bravery Sciences Institute look like?"

—DR. CYNTHIA PURY, bravery researcher,
professor of psychology, Clemson University

"Jill Schulman's *The Bravery Effect* is a masterclass in leveraging discomfort to unlock your full potential. Through powerful storytelling and science-backed insights, she demonstrates that everything we want—success, fulfillment, and impact—is on the other side of challenge. This book is not just a guide; it's a wake-up call to stop playing small and start living boldly. If you're ready to break free from limitations and lead with courage, this is the book you need."

—DAVID MELTZER, legendary sports executive,
speaker, and best-selling author

THE
BRAVERY
EFFECT

THE
BRAVERY
EFFECT

A PARABLE TEACHING *the* SCIENCE
of CONQUERING FEAR, ACHIEVING MORE,
and LIVING LIFE *to the* FULLEST

JILL SCHULMAN

GREENLEAF
BOOK GROUP PRESS

Published by Greenleaf Book Group Press
Austin, Texas
www.gbgpress.com

Distributed by Greenleaf Book Group

For ordering information or special discounts for bulk purchases, please contact Greenleaf Book Group at PO Box 91869, Austin, TX 78709, 512.891.6100.

Design and composition by Greenleaf Book Group
Cover design by Greenleaf Book Group
Cover images used under license from ©Adobestock.com
Author Photography by Laura Bravo Mertz

Publisher's Cataloging-in-Publication data is available.

Print ISBN: 979-8-88645-396-6

eBook ISBN: 979-8-88645-397-3

To offset the number of trees consumed in the printing of our books, Greenleaf donates a portion of the proceeds from each printing to the Arbor Day Foundation. Greenleaf Book Group has replaced over 50,000 trees since 2007.

Printed in the United States of America on acid-free paper

25 26 27 28 29 30 31 32   10 9 8 7 6 5 4 3 2 1

First Edition

For my daughters, Sydney and Brooke.

CONTENTS

FOREWORD

I am perhaps best known for co-authoring *The One Minute Manager*, a business parable that spent over three years on *The New York Times* bestseller list and has sold over fifteen million copies. What's less well-known is how risky the book seemed at the time.

Business books of the day were dense and academic. They were filled with jargon and case studies. Spencer Johnson and I wanted to create something that people could easily remember and share. But it was a leap of faith, and not everyone thought it was a good one. Some of my academic colleagues laughed at the book and were even a little embarrassed by it.

It took courage to make that leap out of our comfort zone, but that experience taught me a valuable life lesson about the power of being brave.

When I met Jill more than a decade ago, she seemed to intuitively already know that lesson. Her time in the Marine Corps and her research in positive psychology had driven home an important truth: **People rarely fall short because they lack talent or potential.** More often, they get stuck in the "comfort trap"—that safe but limiting space where they play small, avoid risk, and convince themselves that "good enough" is, well, good enough.

In this book, Jill shows you how to break free from the "good enough" trap. It's an important message that has the power to change your life.

Like me, I believe you will see yourself in the story that follows. And like me, I hope you will discover that courage is universal and that leaps of faith can lead to great things. So, read this book, follow its advice, and live your most courageous life!

—**KEN BLANCHARD,** coauthor of *The One Minute Manager*®
and *The Simple Truths of Leadership*

AUTHOR'S NOTE

This book is about overcoming the fears that hold you back from achieving what you truly want. I chose to write it as a parable because stories make complex ideas stick. They help us see ourselves in the lessons, making the science of bravery more accessible—and more powerful—to everyone. I still remember reading powerful business parables like *The Five Dysfunctions of a Team, The One Minute Manager, and The Energy Bus* and the lessons they taught. Great stories stick. They may not list every research study or cite every academic source, but their lessons stay with you—sometimes for a lifetime. That's the power of storytelling. It makes concepts memorable, actionable, and real. And this is why I wrote this book as a fictional story.

But make no mistake: The science is real.

I'm a geek at heart. I love the science of learning, development, and positive psychology. I've spent years immersed in the research, and all the principles and lessons presented in this book are backed by evidence. *The Bravery Effect* draws from psychology, neuroscience, behavioral economics, sociology, and philosophy. When you see yourself in the story that follows, know that you are also seeing the work of some of the best minds in those fields.

If you love digging into research, you'll find a section at the end of this book that acknowledges the thinkers, scientists, and researchers whose work has influenced the Building Bravery framework. This includes the major bodies of research and the experts whose insights shaped the ideas in this book.

If you'd like to bring the principles of this book into both your life and work, start by taking the Bravery Assessment to measure where you are now and identify areas for growth. Then download the Bravery Blueprint for practical strategies to help you strengthen your courage in how you think, what you do, and how you interact with others. Just scan the code below or visit jillschulman.com.

THE BRAVE HABIT

Embracing discomfort can change your life.

That's the "bravery effect," and it is the promise at the heart of this book. A life of more success, deeper fulfillment, and fewer regrets can be found in the challenges we choose to pursue. Success is built in the moments where we step into discomfort, where we push past doubt and into something bigger.

I learned this lesson the hard way.

If you had asked a few of my commanding officers, they would have told you that my journey to become a United States Marine was destined to fail. In fact, they told *me*. Within twenty-four hours of my arrival, in 1992, at just eighteen years old, one of them looked me straight in the eye and said, "You don't have what it takes."

To be fair, this wasn't an unreasonable statement. I'd arrived at the Navy's Reserve Officers Training program (NROTC)—the training ground for some of the toughest military teams in history—dressed like I was headed to a sorority mixer. Picture me: hot pink silk shorts with a matching top, high heels in the same vibrant shade, and long, meticulously manicured nails painted to perfectly match my ensemble. I thought I was projecting confidence and polish. I looked like a stunt double for *Legally Blonde*. Now picture every military film you've ever seen with a screaming drill sergeant, and you get the picture.

Within hours of being told I would fail, I had bitten off my long, manicured nails (they were not regulation, I learned), swapped my high heels for combat boots, and made a decision: I would prove them wrong. It was a rough start to an even rougher journey, and the next few years were anything but easy, but they were transformative. I learned firsthand the power of grit, discipline, and embracing discomfort. I discovered how to set audacious goals, work hard, and push past what I thought was possible. By my senior year, I was leading my NROTC battalion of two hundred other students.

I was nothing short of pathetic when I arrived as a freshman. By the time I returned from Officer Candidate School, I had become a top Marine. Along the way, I learned a singular lesson that would shape the rest of my life. I carried it with me through my military career, into corporate America, into my work as a leadership development consultant, and through my master's degree in applied positive psychology at the University of Pennsylvania. It is, unquestionably, the bridge that connects every stage of my life—it is the tie that binds. And it's the reason this book exists.

THE OTHER SIDE OF HARD

Everything you want in life—success, fulfillment, happiness—lives on the other side of hard. The ability to grow, to reach new levels, to become more than you are today requires stepping outside of what's familiar and easy.

In the military, this truth is everywhere. I spent my years in the Marine Corps being uncomfortable, but that was the expectation. Growth through discomfort was part of the culture. As Admiral Nimitz said about the Corps in World War II, "Uncommon valor was a common virtue."[1] Marines don't just accept difficulty; they embrace it, because they know that when you reach the other side of something really hard, you come back stronger and more confident. Or, as we say in the Marine Corps: Pain is weakness leaving the body.

It wasn't until I studied positive psychology that I realized this lesson isn't just for the military. My research showed that discomfort and growth aren't just connected in extreme environments—they are universal. It matters for everyone. I saw real scientific evidence that discomfort and growth weren't things the Marine Corps had invented. All growth—and, by extension, success and happiness—requires leaving your comfort zone. Discomfort is the price of progress. It is a fundamental fact of life: Discomfort and growth are two sides of the same coin. If you want to grow, if you want to achieve more, if you want to live a life without regret, you must get uncomfortable.

> To be successful, you need to grow. To grow, you need to face discomfort.

---

1   Chester Nimitz, "Famous Navy Quotations," Naval History and Heritage Command, July 1, 2024, https://www.history.navy.mil/browse-by-topic/heritage/famous-navy-quotations.html.

To be successful, you need to grow. To grow, you need to face discomfort.

It turns out that almost everything you really want, as you'll see in the pages ahead, is on the other side of something hard.

THE COMFORT TRAP

All around us, however, the world has been going in the opposite direction. The more I work with my corporate clients, the more I realize just how much the workplace is trying to eliminate discomfort. Well-intentioned leaders lower standards and remove challenges, believing this will make people happier and more productive. The same seems true of our homes and schools. Parents and teachers rush to solve children's problems, depriving them of valuable learning experiences. Somehow, as the ultramarathoner Dean Karnazes puts it, "We seem to have confused comfort with happiness."[2] In our families, in our personal lives, and in our work, we have come to believe that discomfort is something to be avoided. It's a pathology, an unwelcome presence to be removed. All the best science tells us that this is simply not true. Seeking comfort to escape what we fear doesn't make life better; it makes life smaller. It is not only the fast lane to an unfulfilling life—it's a *trap*.

All growth happens outside your comfort zone. If you never leave it, you miss out on one of the greatest human abilities: to face adversity and adapt. This principle is perfectly illustrated by how our bodies respond to physical challenge. When we avoid physical exertion—taking the elevator instead of stairs, driving instead of

---

2   Dean Karnazes, *Ultramarathon Man* (Hachette Books, 2023).

walking—our muscles atro-
phy and our cardiovascular
system weakens. If we don't
lift weights and deliberately
stress our muscles and bones,
they gradually become weaker
and more fragile, increasing

> All growth happens outside your comfort zone. If you never leave it, you miss out on one of the greatest human abilities: to face adversity and adapt.

our risk of injury and limiting our capabilities. The less we challenge
our bodies, the less capable they become. The same is true for our
mental and emotional resilience. To always avoid challenge is to be
ensnared by the comfort trap—and the more we avoid challenge,
the weaker we become, and the tighter the trap becomes and the
harder it is to break free.

For most of human history, this trap couldn't exist. Being comfortable all the time simply wasn't an option if you wanted to survive.
You had to face cold, effort, uncertainty, and even danger to get what
you wanted. But today, prosperity and technology have made it easier
than ever to stay comfortable—to shrink away from challenge instead
of stepping into it—thus ensnaring us in the comfort trap.

The solution isn't to remove discomfort; it's to embrace it, seeking out challenges instead of hiding from them. We must build a
habit of running toward the things that scare us rather than away.
Get comfortable being uncomfortable. Become, in a word, *brave.*

THE HABIT OF BEING BRAVE

The challenge is that this can feel terrifying. Ask someone to be
brave, and they often imagine dramatic, high-stakes moments like
rushing into a burning building, standing in front of a charging

enemy, or risking everything on a business idea. But bravery isn't only about grand, cinematic gestures; it's about the small, everyday choices we make. It's saying yes to a stretch assignment at work when your inner critic says you're not ready. It's raising your hand in a meeting to share an idea that might get challenged. It's deciding to have the uncomfortable conversation you've been avoiding, or to apply for the promotion even though you might not get it. These are the kinds of moments that shape who we become.

Let me dispel a few myths about bravery that might be holding you back. The first is the belief that bravery is a rare, once-in-a-lifetime act. Courage isn't just for first responders, soldiers, or extreme athletes. It's in the choices we make every day—setting a goal that stretches us, speaking up when it matters, taking action before we feel ready. Bravery isn't the absence of fear, but the willingness to move forward despite it. And the more we practice it, the more natural it becomes.

The second myth is that bravery is something you either have or you don't. But bravery isn't something you're born with; it's something you develop. The ability to embrace discomfort—and grow because of it—is a trainable skill, a mindset, and a practice. Just as with physical fitness, our capacity for bravery follows predictable patterns. When you first start lifting weights, you begin with what you can handle. Gradually, you add weight as your muscles adapt and strengthen. The same principle applies to bravery. The more we lean into discomfort, the stronger and more capable we become. Every day presents dozens of small chances to be brave—to take a risk, to stand up for someone, to push ourselves beyond what feels safe. And each time we step up, we build a life of greater confidence, success, and fulfillment.

Bravery isn't just about bold, heroic acts; it's about refusing to let fear dictate your choices. And when we do that, something powerful happens—we unlock agency. With each brave choice, we shift from being passive passengers in our own lives to becoming the captains. Rather than drifting wherever circumstances take us, we begin charting our own course. We stop merely reacting to life and start intentionally creating it.

Conquering the fear that holds us back is what this book is all about, but not all fear is bad. Some fear is protective—it keeps us from walking alone at night in unsafe places, getting too close to the edge of a cliff, or gambling away our savings. That fear is wise. But the fear of being judged, rejected, or failing at something that matters? That's the fear that deserves to be challenged. That's the fear that keeps us small and prevents us from becoming the best version of ourselves.

This is the heart of it: To be brave is to be willing to face—and embrace—discomfort. It's as simple as that. Running into burning buildings or standing up to injustice are also forms of courage, but when we take courageous action toward *anything* that matters— even when it scares us—we become brave. Every day, we are given dozens of small opportunities to be brave in life and work. Every day, those opportunities can reward us in astonishing ways, if we are willing to step up to them.

And let's be clear—bravery is not bravado. This isn't about recklessness or doing hard things just to prove a point. This is about finding the edge of your discomfort—the zone where growth lives. Think of it like Goldilocks and the

> To be brave is to be willing to face—and embrace—discomfort.

three bears—there's a sweet spot we're aiming for. Too little challenge leads to boredom and stagnation. Too much could lead to anxiety or burnout. The goal is to find that "just right" zone where you're stretching beyond comfort but not breaking. Difficult, but doable—that's where the transformation happens.

You know that feeling, when something challenges you and scares you because it might be hard or you might fail, but it excites you because achieving it would be deeply meaningful? That simultaneous fear and excitement is your compass pointing toward growth. Not all fear is bad. But the fears that hold you back from pursuing what you truly want—those are the ones we'll learn to face and move beyond.

I discovered that embracing challenge was the key to unlocking higher levels of success, fulfillment, and happiness. Yet so many of us feel stuck. We are held back by fear, hesitation, or the comfort of what is familiar. We want to be braver, but we don't always know how.

Bravery is a highly desirable trait but isn't something we are simply born with. It's a skill that can be built, practiced, and strengthened. Like any worthwhile skill, it requires consistency—fifteen minutes of brave action daily will transform you more profoundly than fifteen hours once a year. Like physical training, it's not the occasional sprint that builds endurance—it's the daily reps that change you. That is why I wrote this book: to show you that bravery isn't out of reach. It's already within you, waiting to be developed. Bravery is one of the character strengths people most wish to develop,[3] yet

---

3   Ryan Niemiec, "Mental Health and Character Strengths: The Dual Role of Boosting Well-Being and Reducing Suffering," *Mental Health and Social Inclusion* 27, no. 4 (November 30, 2023): 294–316, https://doi.org/10.1108/MHSI-01-2023-0012.

many of us feel stuck in our comfort zones; we don't know how to be braver. This book will change that.

You may never rush into a burning building to save a life, but bravery isn't just for extreme moments. Every day, you are given the chance to be brave—to push yourself outside your comfort zone, to speak up when it matters, to take on a challenge that stretches you. These seemingly small choices compound over time, shaping your confidence and success and the impact you make in the world.

That's the transformation I want for you. Bravery isn't about waiting for the perfect moment; it's about taking action, again and again, until courageous becomes who you are. That's what this book will help you do.

For thousands of years, philosophers have taught that bravery is the key to a meaningful life. Today, science is proving them right. Research in psychology, neuroscience, and behavioral economics confirms what the Stoics, warriors, and great thinkers have always known: Without courage, success is limited, happiness is fleeting, and regret becomes inevitable.

Bravery isn't just a virtue—it's a requirement for anyone who wants to achieve more, experience deeper fulfillment, and live without looking back in disappointment. The bravery effect is the way courageous thoughts, actions, and relationships enrich our lives. The cost of inaction is high. Avoiding challenges, shrinking from discomfort, or hesitating in fear doesn't keep you safe—it guarantees a life of missed opportunities.

> **Bravery isn't about waiting for the perfect moment; it's about taking action, again and again, until courageous becomes who you are.**

The ideas that follow are built on both timeless wisdom and modern science—not just theories, but proven truths about how people grow, push past fear, and create lives they're proud of. The choice is always there: Step forward into courage or stay stuck and wonder what could have been.

You may have picked up this book seeking greater achievement and success—and the science of bravery will certainly deliver that. But here's the deeper truth: It's not about the accomplishments themselves. The medals, promotions, or accolades are merely byproducts. What truly matters is who you become on the journey of overcoming your fears. With each brave step, you forge a stronger, more resilient, more capable version of yourself. The real transformation happens within—in the quiet pride of knowing you didn't back down, in the deep satisfaction of pushing past your limits, in the profound self-trust that develops when you prove to yourself, again and again, that you can do hard things. This internal transformation is the true gift of bravery—it changes how you see yourself, and consequently how you move through the world. And that changes everything.

As a leadership consultant, I've seen firsthand the effects of bravery, how it transforms organizations—driving innovation, building stronger teams, and unlocking potential. As a mother of two daughters, I see an even deeper truth: Bravery isn't just about leadership; it's about life. The ability to embrace discomfort, face fear, and take bold action isn't just a professional advantage—it's the foundation of growth, resilience, and fulfillment. You deserve this gift.

The truths in this book are universal. They shape how we lead, how we parent, how we show up in our relationships, and how we navigate challenges. They have the power to reshape your story. Bravery doesn't just create success—it creates well-being, purpose, and a life without regret.

The world needs more brave people.

My job is to convince you that you're one of them.

—JILL SCHULMAN

THE
BRAVERY
EFFECT

ONE

MISERY AT 35,000 FEET

*L*adies and gentlemen, the captain has turned on the seat belt sign—

Alex tried to ignore the announcement. He was well aware of the turbulence, thank you very much. Besides, his seat belt was already so tight it hurt. On his tray table, he watched ripples dance across his untouched champagne. He wondered—yet again—if business class had been a bad idea.

Of course it was a bad idea, a voice in his head said. *Yet one more in a series.*

He snuck a glance at the woman beside him and felt a pang of envy. She was engrossed in a book, oblivious to the bumpy flight. *How do people do it?*

Then the plane lurched again, sending his stomach into anxious somersaults.

———

The trouble had started long before the flight.

When the invitation to his fraternity reunion arrived, it had sounded like the perfect getaway. A weekend back at his alma mater, reconnecting with old friends, cutting loose; what could be better?

For months, Alex had felt like a drowning man struggling to keep his head above a rising tide of work. Some days, he'd sit at his desk, chest tight, convinced he might suffocate under the sheer weight of it all.

Like right now, he thought grimly, as he cranked his seat belt tighter.

It's not the workload, he thought. *You're bored—not from too little work but from too little that excites you.*

It was true. The year before, he had been offered a dream job—a key role that he'd coveted for nearly half a decade.

And he'd turned it down.

Why?

You chickened out, he thought.

It was harsh, but true. The dream job came with one nightmare component: He would have to fly regularly, and Alex had been terrified of flying since traveling as an unaccompanied twelve-year-old on a particularly bad flight.

The idea of doing it every other week? Impossible.

So instead, he took what he thought was the safer move—transferring to Keeling's product-development team. It wasn't a promotion, but it wasn't a step backward, either.

Now, a year later, it felt like quicksand.

The core team was disengaged. Every new idea was killed on arrival. The five-person team felt like it was perpetually on the verge of one crisis or another.

But the worst part wasn't the dysfunction. It was the stagnation.

Alex had always been the guy pushing forward, leading, solving problems. Now, he felt like an engine stuck in neutral: revving but going nowhere.

And it wasn't just at work.

At home, he felt disconnected from his wife, Maggie. Most nights, he barely made it home in time to say goodnight to their son, Trevor, and sneak a peek at Zoey, their sleeping toddler.

A voice in his head kept whispering in his mind over the past months: *You're missing it, Alex.*

That's why the reunion seemed like the perfect reset. Maggie had encouraged him to take the trip, of course. And he'd agreed, despite his misgivings about the flight, which he'd tried not to think about. He focused instead on how the weekend away would change things. He'd come back recharged, filled with new ideas, new energy. He'd come back *inspired.*

Instead, it had done the opposite. Alex hadn't left the reunion feeling motivated. Everywhere he'd turned, his former classmates seemed to be thriving. For three days, he'd experienced something closer to *envy.* His first college roommate, Dylan, was now, against all odds, an investment banker. He seemed to be jetting everywhere. Everyone he met seemed to be so successful, so happy, so healthy.

Was he feeling jealous?

Maybe a little. But there was more to it. He didn't begrudge his friends their success. What nagged at him was how passionate everyone seemed about their work and life. How engaged. They seemed to be accomplishing so much. If he was jealous of anything, it wasn't their income—it was their impact.

After college, Alex had taken what seemed like the perfect opportunity: a good, entry-level job with a stable company. Plenty of room to move up.

Meanwhile, guys like Dylan had taken risks. Some had launched businesses. Some had job hopped, chasing bigger opportunities.

And now, looking back, *They have all lapped me. What happened to me?*

When Alex finally left the reunion and headed to the airport, what he felt was loss. What had happened to the old Alex? The go-getter with a million ideas? He thought of his young son Trevor, who was never short of ideas. What was the word Trevor loved? *Lame.*

Have I become lame?

Maybe that explained why he'd spent his limited savings on this pointless business class upgrade.

You're trying to feel successful, he thought bitterly.

He had also hoped the extra space, the quieter cabin, and, if he was being honest, the free alcohol might take the edge off his fear of flying. Maybe he'd even enjoy the flight.

How wrong he'd been.

Business class wasn't the luxurious oasis he'd imagined. The cabin seemed just as claustrophobic as economy. And his stomach was tied so tightly he hadn't even had a sip of his champagne. The glass just sat there, shimmering, threatening to spill with each jolt of the plane. A reminder that he was strapped inside a gigantic metal tube hurling through the sky, thousands of feet above the earth.

If enjoying a flight meant your brain screaming *don't die don't die don't die* . . . well, mission accomplished.

Almost as if the pilot was listening, the aircraft started juddering through the sky, each jarring bump making the overhead compartments rattle and the seat belt dig into Alex's waist. Alex gripped the armrest like it was his last moment on earth.

"Are you okay?"

Alex flinched at the voice. He looked up, expecting the flight attendant. But it wasn't.

The steady, warm voice had come from the woman beside him, in 2A. She had the window seat. Alex, of course, had chosen the aisle. Some primitive part of his brain had decided that if the plane slammed into the earth at 800 mph, he would be better off closer to the exit. He realized she had set her book down and was waiting for a reply.

"Just feeling uncomfortable," Alex said. His voice was thin and tight.

He turned his head stiffly toward her. The woman's eyes flicked down to where his hands were gripping the armrest.

"Lucky you," she said.

Alex blinked. "Pardon me?"

Did she just say I was lucky?

"Being uncomfortable," she said. "That's fortunate."

Alex gave her a bewildered look. This woman is out of her mind.

"I used to be terrified of flying," she continued, unbothered by his reaction. "It was the best thing that ever happened to me."

Best thing? Alex stared at her, as she seemed like she enjoyed turbulence.

"I know it's hard," she said. "In my line of work, we say, 'Everything you want is on the other side of something uncomfortable.'"

Alex had no idea what she meant, but he realized she was looking at him with genuine concern. He seized on her attention like it was a dangling oxygen mask.

"What kind of work do you do?" he managed to ask.

The woman tilted her head slightly, studying him. There was no judgment in her gaze, and Alex felt his insides relax a little further. She was, he realized, strangely *calming*—somehow both relaxed and entirely confident at the same time. *There's something compelling about her*, he thought.

"I help people get uncomfortable," she answered.

The statement was so unexpected that, for a moment, Alex forgot that he was strapped into a tin can hurtling through the air.

"What does that mea—"

The plane shuddered violently, cutting him off. *Oh God,* he thought.

The woman beside him didn't flinch.

"Do you have family here?" the woman asked, casually shifting the subject.

Grateful for the distraction, Alex told the woman about his wife, Maggie, and the kids.

She nodded. "I have a husband and two daughters—almost grown up now. My husband is meeting me in arrivals," she said. "I travel a lot for work, but he always picks me up. It's a nice way to come home."

She was terrified of flying . . . but traveled for work?

Alex couldn't imagine it.

The bumpy weather continued for the rest of the flight.

Alex spent the last twenty minutes of the flight simply holding on for dear life. The woman in 2A didn't try to reassure him again, and Alex didn't expect her to. But as the plane rocked sideways in the crosswinds, he would've gratefully accepted it if she had.

Then, with a final jarring jolt, it was over. They were on the ground. Minutes later, they were at their gate. The seat belt sign dinged off. Alex was immediately on his feet, pulling his suitcase from the overhead bin, his mind laser focused on escape.

As he lowered his case to the floor, he caught the eye of the woman in 2A. She was still calm, smiling pleasantly. It was hard to imagine that she had once been afraid of flying.

"It was nice to meet you," Alex stammered. "I'm sorry it wasn't under better circumstances."

The woman tilted her head to the side again, as if considering his words.

"Be careful what you wish for," she said.

Again, Alex was confused. *Maybe part of business class is sitting beside people who speak in riddles*, he thought.

The woman smiled and handed him a business card. Then she effortlessly hoisted her carry-on out of the overhead bin.

"Congratulations on a tough flight," she said.

Then she was gone.

Alex stuffed the business card in his pocket and walked off the plane, almost immediately forgetting the woman in 2A in the overwhelming relief of solid ground.

———

As his rideshare exited the freeway, just blocks from home, Alex's mind began to settle into a state that he knew too well: *dread.*

Tomorrow was another day.

The weekend was supposed to recharge him, but instead, he felt drained. Not just from the flight—though that had been miserable—but from everything. He had thought the reunion would ignite something in him, a spark that he desperately needed. A sense of excitement. Instead, he was coming home exhausted, jittery from adrenaline, and even more discouraged than ever.

He had missed a whole weekend with Trevor and Zoey, and for what? To feel worse?

And then there was Maggie.

She'd had high hopes too. She'd encouraged him to go, believing he'd return rejuvenated. That he'd come back better. But the thought of waking up tomorrow to face another day of work left him feeling empty. What was the point? The team was getting nowhere. The prototype wasn't working—that much was obvious.

He was showing up every day, to get nowhere. Meanwhile, his friends were out there building things. Creating things. Making a difference.

And he was just . . . stuck. Alex slumped deeper into his seat. *Try to see the positive,* he thought. It was something Maggie always said. More often, lately. She was his rock, the person who always seemed to have faith in him. In everything. He knew he should listen to her.

But how?

The house was dark when Alex let himself in. He emptied his pockets onto the entryway table—the usual pile of keys, wallet, and loose change, plus the crumpled business card from the woman in 2A. He'd forgotten about that.

Be careful what you wish for.

The words drifted through his mind. He still didn't understand what she'd meant. Shaking it off, he headed for the kitchen. Maggie was probably sound asleep. There was a note on the kitchen counter:

Welcome home!
I can't wait to hear all about your trip.

—Love you, Mags xo

He ran a thumb over the paper.

This was one of the things he loved most about Maggie—how she always made him feel wanted, like he belonged. She was so caring. So considerate. He'd suggested she join him on the trip since a few of the wives were joining, but Maggie insisted he make this about *him*, not them.

"I'll be fine," she'd said. "Besides, these are *your* old friends from college. I don't want you focused on making sure I am having fun. Enjoy them."

It all made sense, but Alex couldn't help but wonder if money had played a part in her decision. That left a sour taste in his mouth.

Turbulence.

Not the kind in the air. The kind that crept into their lives. Subtle at first: small worries about finances and his career. About their future.

These thoughts made his stomach clench again, like he was back at 35,000 feet. He sighed and ran his fingers through his hair. Tomorrow, he'd have to be up early, back to the office, back to the grind. Back to a life that felt more and more like flying: overwhelming and completely out of his control.

Before heading to bed, Alex padded softly down the hall and opened the door to Trevor's room. His ten-year-old son was sprawled across the bed, blankets twisted around him, sleeping deeply.

Alex's heart swelled. *He's changing so fast.*

Next, he peeked into Zoey's room. The door was slightly ajar, just the way she liked it. He could see her cuddled up with her favorite stuffed animal, Dumbo.

Alex smiled. He'd bought that for her the last time they went to Disneyland. She'd clung to it ever since, carrying it everywhere, even after the trip was just a memory. He loved that she loved it so much.

It seemed like only yesterday he and Maggie had repainted the nursery rose pink, preparing for her arrival. Now, the tiny blonde bundle of energy was old enough to start preschool.

Where is the time going?

For a long moment, he just stood there, listening to her steady, even breaths. Minutes later, Alex slipped into bed beside Maggie. As had happened every night for weeks, his mind immediately turned to work. A sudden urge to escape hit him. But escape what, exactly?

That was the problem. It was hard to escape if you didn't know what you were trying to escape from. All Alex knew was that some part of him seemed to be slowly slipping away. Somewhere along the way, he'd gone from captain to passenger in his own life. Days, weeks, months—they all blurred together, carrying him along like a leaf in a current. He wasn't steering anymore; he was just . . . drifting. Watching as life happened around him, to him, despite him. The worst part was feeling powerless to change course, as if the rudder had broken off long ago and he'd only just noticed.

This isn't me.

He was exhausted, but his thoughts kept him awake. Eventually, his exhaustion won out, and he drifted into a restless sleep—one filled with images of planes, of falling, and of a mysterious woman who kept congratulating him for being terrified.

TWO

SOLID GROUND

Alex woke before his alarm and slipped quietly from bed. Maggie and the kids were still asleep. Moving carefully, he gathered some clothes in the dark and eased out of the room.

They would be disappointed to find him gone: Maggie would want to hear a debrief of his trip, and the kids would be eager to have him back in their morning routine. But he simply couldn't face the conversation. Not yet.

He could already hear Maggie's gentle but pointed questions about the business class ticket. The expense had been unnecessary, and they both knew it. But that wasn't the real reason for avoiding her. What he couldn't bear was explaining to Maggie just how small he felt after spending the weekend with his successful peers.

Besides, Maggie had concerns of her own. She loved the performing arts charter school she taught at, and Alex knew she was exceptionally talented, but little had changed in recent years. She was due for a shift, and Alex sensed she was holding back. Not for the first time, he wondered if Maggie felt just as disengaged as he did.

Alex had noticed the stack of education journals on her night-stand growing taller, her late-night browsing of university programs when she thought he wasn't paying attention. Just yesterday, he'd overheard her on the phone with a former professor, discussing "the-oretical frameworks" and "doctoral programs." He pretended not to notice, but he wondered if her dreams were expanding beyond the classroom—and whether she, like him, was afraid to pursue them.

And then there was Paris.

Maggie had raised the subject again before Alex had left on his trip. It was another long-overdue conversation, but he wasn't ready for that today, either. Especially with the anxious memory of the flight still lingering.

Instead, he was determined to start fresh at work. *I'll get an early start this morning,* he thought. *Get caught up on the work I missed.*

Alex had just finished his coffee when Trevor entered the room in his pajamas, his hair sticking out in all directions.

"Hey, kiddo," he said. "You're up early."

Trevor's eyes lit up. "You're home!" He ran to Alex.

This never gets old, Alex thought, gratefully accepting the hug.

"Can you stay home with me?"

Alex laughed. "I wish, kiddo, but I have to get to work. And you need to get to school."

He watched as a cloud seemed to pass over Trevor's face.

"What's up?" Alex asked.

Trevor shrugged, then wandered into the kitchen and pulled a box of cereal from the cupboard.

That's odd. Alex considered pressing the issue, but before he could, his phone buzzed in his pocket. He retrieved his phone and quickly glanced at the screen. It was an email from work. *Strange to get something from the office this early,* Alex thought, then tucked the phone away. *Tonight,* he promised himself. I'll talk to him tonight.

Alex plucked his car keys from the hall table where he had emptied his pockets the night before. He noticed the crumpled business card the woman in 2A had handed him.

"Lucky you," she had said.

Alex shook his head as he walked out the front door.

———

He felt his spirits lift ever so slightly as he pulled into the parking lot. His early start had meant no traffic. That gave him time to stop for his favorite coffee. *So far so good.*

Alex looked at the coffee cup, and an image flashed in his mind of his former boss and mentor, Carter. Carter *loved* coffee. He had told Alex it was his greatest decision-making tool. "When in doubt," Carter would say, "caffeinate and think it through."

Alex was in doubt a lot lately. He often found himself asking, *What would Carter do?* More than once, in recent weeks, he had wished he could actually speak to the man. But Carter was a busy executive, and Alex no longer worked for him.

Yet here he was, at the office early, coffee in hand. *You can still caffeinate and think it through,* he thought. He could catch up on his missed work and be ready to hit the ground running at 8 a.m. This, Alex decided, was how he would turn things around. A new routine was exactly what he needed: wake up earlier, beat the traffic to work. Get a head start on the day.

A voice in his head interrupted. *Haven't you tried this all before?* Alex ignored the voice. *This time would be different.*

The sun began to clear the low buildings that housed the offices of the Keeling Group, and for the first time since the flight home, Alex thought maybe the weekend away and the business class ticket hadn't been such a bad investment after all. As he parked, he noticed there were other cars in the lot. That was a surprise. He had expected it to be practically empty this early in the day.

He swiped his key card to enter the employee entrance, then made his way inside. As he walked toward his office, he heard several voices carrying from ahead. *Strange.* It was too early for a big meeting.

Rounding the corner, he stopped short. He found the source of the voices. The large glass-walled meeting room near the lobby was filled—a dozen or more people inside. And they weren't just having a meeting.

Even through the thick glass, Alex could hear raised voices and see red faces. Animated gestures. This kind of body language meant the conversation was anything but calm.

Alex frowned. Something else was off. Alex didn't recognize most of the people. At least half of the red faces belonged to people in suits he had never seen before.

What the hell was going on?

As he continued past, the raised voices faded, and his thoughts turned to his day.

First, email, he thought. *Then I'll get organized. I'll finally get that costing done on the prototype. I'll reach out to the potential vendor.*

He felt another quiver of optimism. Maybe everything would be okay. Maybe getting back to work—really digging in—would help him shake the restless, sinking feeling.

THREE

TROUBLE ON THE HORIZON

None of it went according to plan.

Alex had been at his desk for less than five minutes when he heard a sharp tap on the glass window of his office. He looked up to see Nico peering in. He barely resisted the urge to sigh.

Nico was his immediate boss, the head of the development team. He was tall, nearly gaunt, with a nervous energy about him. He always seemed a little breathless, always moving like he was late for something. And strangely *shiny*, as if he were perpetually coated in a thin layer of sweat.

He wore a similar outfit almost every day: a tucked-in button-down shirt, pressed slacks, and polished brown shoes. Impeccably neat, almost too neat—as if the routine helped him keep chaos at bay. His collar was just a bit too stiff, and his smartwatch blinked nonstop with reminders and alerts. He moved through the office like a wind-up toy wound one click too tight, walking fast, always darting from place to place like he was late for a meeting no one else had on their calendar.

You could tell he tried to control the variables he could—his schedule, his clothes, his pace—even if his energy (and his sweat) gave away the rest.

Maggie had met him once, during an off-site social event. She had whispered in Alex's ear within five minutes of meeting him: "Did he jog here?" That was just Nico. Precise. Worried. A little shiny. And right now, looking even more frantic than usual.

Alex gestured toward his open laptop as if to say, *I'm busy*. Nico bobbed his head up and down in rapid agreement but tapped his thin wrist.

Nico poked his head in. "I sent an email early this morning," he said, slightly out of breath. "We've got a meeting in five minutes." Alex frowned. He recalled the extra cars in the parking lot and the heated meeting he had seen earlier. He had a bad feeling in his gut.

Something is up.

With another sigh, Alex closed his laptop. So much for caffeinating and thinking it through. Catching up—if that was something that even existed—was going to have to wait.

Fifteen minutes later, Alex was walking toward the shared meeting space used by the development team. It was still early, and he already felt drained.

When he'd started at Keeling, he'd been energized. Plenty of mornings, he woke up before his alarm clock, eager to dive in. There was momentum, a sense of purpose. He felt like his work mattered.

Now? That feeling had vanished. He felt like a cog in a stalled-out machine. The development team—what should have been the beating heart of innovation—was stagnant. Every idea was dismissed as too risky, too different, or too "resource intensive."

Alex thought being organized and doing everything by the book was fine, but Nico's leadership seemed to be leading them . . . well, nowhere. The team had been at a standstill for months. How was the development team supposed to succeed if they never *developed* anything?

Now, as if to illustrate the point, Nico's gaunt face peered anxiously through the glass at him.

Alex exhaled sharply. It's just another Monday. Get through the meeting. Get your work done. He pushed open the door.

There were three people in the room—the core of the development team, minus Willow.

Nico looked up from his laptop, looking frazzled. "Does anyone know where Willow is?"

"Ten minutes late, as always," came a muffled voice.

The voice belonged to Raj, a stout man in his thirties who sat directly across from Alex, laptop open, pen and paper neatly squared, ready for business. His polo shirt was tucked with military precision, and his desk setup looked like it had been measured with a ruler—twice. Even his coffee mug sat perfectly centered on its coaster. His haircut was crisp, his shave flawless, like he approached grooming the same way he approached spreadsheets: with structure and no margin for error.

Raj was a rule-follower, a systems guy. The kind of person who read the user manual before plugging something in, and then highlighted it. He thrived on clarity and order and had little tolerance for people who threw off the rhythm. He was the by-the-book guy, which was why he had little patience for Willow's chronic tardiness.

Beside Raj sat Mo, universally beloved. Mo was always cheerful, always kind. He moved through any space with an easy, lumbering warmth. He was a gentle giant, slightly round, with thick, dark curls that blended into his full and well-kept beard. His eyes twinkled beneath heavy brows, always reflecting the warmth of his ever-present smile. Mo wasn't a productivity powerhouse, but he was so likable that no one ever called him out on it.

Alex took his usual seat across from Raj, who was lightly tapping his index finger on the edge of his laptop. Like the rest of them, he knew something was up.

"Well, we'll have to get started without Willow," Nico said.

"What's going on?" Raj said abruptly. "I saw the board members leaving the building as I arrived."

So that's who that was, Alex thought.

"And they didn't leave us any donuts?" Mo joked.

Most days, Mo's comment would have lifted the room. Today, the joke fell flat.

"I know some of you have heard rumors," Nico said. "And, give or take a few details, they are true."

No one spoke.

What rumors? Alex thought. *What did I miss while I was gone?*

"In a nutshell," Nico continued, "the company is getting ready to make some tough financial decisions. We've lost market share to smaller, more nimble firms who have been able to convert our customers to theirs. To stay financially healthy, we need to cut costs."

Raj's finger tapped a little faster.

"Unfortunately," Nico continued, "our division has not significantly contributed to profitability. And our trends . . . aren't very promising."

Raj stiffened. "Are we losing our jobs?" His voice had risen in pitch.

Alex felt his stomach clench again, and his mind began to spin with thoughts of their mortgage and the car payment. The college funds. The bills they always seemed just barely able to pay.

"No," Nico said.

Raj exhaled and visibly relaxed.

Nico hesitated. "Not yet, at least."

Raj's face fell again.

"This morning, the board held an emergency meeting to decide next steps," Nico said.

Silence.

Raj couldn't contain himself. "*And?*" he blurted out.

Nico swallowed hard. His face somehow looked shinier than before.

"We've been asked to prepare a plan . . . for winding down the division."

The room was dead silent. Then everyone began talking at once.

"Wait," Raj said, his voice rising above the rest. "That's it? No other options? What does 'winding down' even mean?"

"The CEO and the board have made their decision," Nico said, his voice steady but heavy. "After reviewing every possible option, they believe the only viable path forward is to shut down our division. Liquidating our assets will provide the cash flow the company desperately needs to stay afloat. From a financial standpoint, they see no other choice."

He glanced down at his notes, then looked up, hesitating for a moment before adding, "Or, as one board member put it"—he held up his fingers in air quotes—"'unless someone comes up with a miracle.'"

FOUR

PUSHBACK

N o one spoke.

The silence was so profound that Alex could hear the distant hum of the mechanical room and the faint *shhhh* of circulating air.

And under that, he could hear the rapid thump of his own heartbeat.

Am I going to lose my job?

Just hours before, he had wanted to step back, reduce his workload. But not to zero! His mind began to spin. What would he tell Maggie? How would they make ends meet? Save for college?

He scanned the room.

Raj, pale faced, had stopped tapping his finger. He was, it seemed, done processing. Mo had a stunned grin plastered to his face, the kind people wore when they couldn't quite process the bad news yet.

Alex swallowed. If anything, Raj's panic made Alex feel better. *Get a grip*, he thought. *Raj has two kids. Nico's on the stretch to retirement.*

Alex set aside his fears and tuned his attention back to Nico. "What about the prototype?"

Mo let out a short laugh. "Given what we've accomplished in the last six months, the prototype is *years* from market. We would be lucky to get a budget approved in six months, never mind *make* something."

Nico nodded. "Given the current state of the prototype—and the funding constraints—the board is probably right."

Mo leaned back in his chair and smirked. "Unless someone has that miracle in their back pocket."

The room was silent. Then, after a beat, Mo shrugged and said, "Or . . . could we?" His voice carried a hint of mischief, but there was something else there too—a flicker of possibility.

Raj exhaled sharply. "I am not comfortable with this. There's no way we can turn things around that quickly."

Part of Alex was desperate to embrace some kind of escape. *Maybe they're right,* he thought. Maybe this is over.

Nico continued, his voice flat, almost resigned. "My recommendation is that we prepare a plan to slash expenses and liquidate all inventory over the coming six months. I'll bring it to the board and get the green light for a structured, safe shutdown of the division. We can recoup some losses and put ourselves in a good position to keep our jobs. There's no guarantee, but the board has assured me they'll do their best to place us in other roles across the company."

A collective sigh of relief rippled through the room.

"I can get a slide deck started," Raj said.

Nico nodded, making a note.

"Happy to help," Mo chimed in. "Tell me what you need."

Alex watched, uncertain, as the team got to work.

Thirty minutes later, they had outlined a plan in place to build a presentation to the board outlining a clear dissolution of the division over six months. Even Raj was on board, offering concise suggestions to make their presentation more impactful.

Alex contributed almost nothing.

Something about the conversation wasn't sitting right. On the surface, it made sense. The numbers were clear. Times were tough. Innovation took time and money. What more could they do?

Maybe Nico is right, he thought. *There's no way we can fix this.*

Still, something nagged at him.

But as the meeting wrapped up, his thoughts drifted to more pressing matters. He was already going to have to tell Maggie that his weekend away had failed *and* left them with a sizable credit card balance. Now, he would have to tell her that he was about to lose his job.

As he left the building, Alex met Willow at the door.

"What's wrong?" she said.

Alex paused.

"Your face," she clarified. "Are you okay?"

She doesn't know, Alex thought.

In contrast to her name, Willow was anything but willowy. She was young, and Alex knew she had received a full athletic scholarship to college. She had the strong build of an athlete and was one of the few people Alex knew who actually used the company gym. Her posture still carried the discipline of a former team captain—shoulders back, chin up, always ready to move.

Tall and naturally confident, she favored tailored slacks, solid blouses, and practical flats, partly because she was always in motion, and partly because she didn't feel the need to add height to a frame that already made her stand out. Her hair was always pulled back into a clean ponytail, and she wore little to no makeup, exuding a kind of effortless competence. She never stayed seated for long.

Keeling was her first job. She was enthusiastic, and Alex appreciated her energy. Sometimes she was late, sometimes she missed the nuance of office politics—but she made up for it with effort, optimism, and a kind of unshakable sincerity. What he liked best, however, was that Willow was naturally great with people. She had a way of reading the room without trying, and knowing what to say—or when to just listen.

He briefed her on the situation.

"Oh my gosh," she said. "How is everyone? How are *you?*"

That's just like Willow, he thought. *Thinking of others first.*

He felt an unexpected urge to tell her the rest of the story. His failed trip. His fear of disappointing Maggie. His sense of disengagement.

Instead, he stuffed it down. There was a job to do. This wasn't about him.

"I'm fine," he lied.

Willow narrowed her eyes, studying him. "Right."

Alex cleared his throat. "I should get going. Nico is looking for you. Big day tomorrow."

Willow continued to study him.

"Okay," she said at last.

———

For the first time in his life, Alex appreciated the rush hour traffic.

He dreaded the conversation that awaited. Even as he pulled into the driveway, he was unsure whether to tell Maggie any of it.

She has enough to worry about, he thought. *Maybe I should just wait until I know more.*

But that didn't feel right, either. Maggie wasn't just his partner; she was his best friend. They had always been good communicators. He already felt guilty that they hadn't discussed his trip, and, truth be told, Alex hadn't been entirely forthcoming about how disengaged he was at work.

Are we drifting apart? he wondered. *Pressure at work is getting to me . . . and I'm bringing it home. I've been short with Maggie. Distant. And I barely see the kids. No wonder things feel off.*

There was more to his reluctance, Alex knew. Maggie had been very supportive of his trip, but he knew she was quietly hoping he would also become more comfortable with flying itself. That would allow them to do some of the traveling that Maggie had always dreamed of. So far, they had spent much of their relationship going to places they could easily drive to. National parks. State capitals.

But those aren't Paris.

Paris was Maggie's bucket list trip. She'd always wanted to go to France. She had family history there. Her great-grandfather had fought at Normandy. She had even been studying French in her spare time. So far, however, the cost of the trip had seemed prohibitive, and Alex wasn't sure he could take more than a week away from work.

But if you were honest, he thought, *you'd tell her you just couldn't bear the thought of such a long flight.*

He sighed and stepped out of the car.

———

He told Maggie everything—almost.

He explained the failed trip and his struggles at work. Feeling uninspired. His sense of spinning his wheels. He finished with the final news: He might lose his job.

He left out Paris.

Through it all, Maggie was silent. She simply listened. When Alex paused, she waited. And then she listened some more. Finally, when he had nothing left to say, she spoke.

"Why do you think you might lose your job?"

Alex shrugged. "The board decided to shut down our division unless we came up with a miracle," he said. "I should start getting my resume together."

Maggie considered this. "It's not possible?"

The question caught Alex off guard. He opened his mouth and then closed it again.

"I mean, I guess it isn't *impossible?*" he said, finally. "I'm just not comfortable with the timeline and deliverables."

This time, it looked like Maggie was the one caught off guard.

"What?" Alex said.

"What did you say?"

"I said I wasn't comfortable—"

Alex broke off as Maggie abruptly stood and left the room.

What?

Moments later, she returned.

"I found this on the hall table this morning," she said. She held out her hand, and Alex recognized the crumpled business card that the woman in 2A had handed him.

"In all the chaos at work I forgot about her!" He shook his head. "That wasn't my proudest moment. I was having a panic attack on the plane, and the woman in the next seat reassured me." He grinned sheepishly at Maggie. "I felt like a four-year-old on my first flight."

"What does she do, exactly?" Maggie handed the card to him. "She has an interesting job title."

Alex read the card:

DR. ANDREA HASTINGS

Founder & Chief Discomfort Officer
BRAVE SCIENCES INSTITUTE

Chief Discomfort Officer? It was the strangest job title he had ever seen. He looked at Maggie and shrugged. "I don't really know," he said. "I was so anxious to get off the flight that I never even looked at the card."

He thought back to the previous day. What had the woman said? The whole experience had been a bit of a blur. Something about helping people or organizations get uncomfortable?

We're already pretty uncomfortable, he thought. *I'm part of a disengaged team facing potential job cuts.*

"What?" Maggie was staring at him.

"I was just thinking that we've had more than enough discomfort already."

Maggie was silent for a moment. She picked up the business card again.

"Maybe you should call her," Maggie said.

"Why?"

"I don't know," Maggie said, "but you're uncomfortable, and apparently she deals with discomfort."

"Do you think she's a therapist?"

"All I know is what you've told me and what's on this card," Maggie said. "She wouldn't have given you her card unless she was open to talking and thought she could help. What's the downside to calling her?"

Maggie squeezed his hand, then stood and planted a kiss on the top of his head.

"I know the trip and your flight home didn't turn out like you'd hoped," she said. "But I want you to know that I think you made the right choice."

"You do?"

"We'll figure out the money," she said. "We always have."

"Thanks," Alex said. "Really." He held up the card. "You think I should call?"

Maggie shrugged. "That's up to you," she said. She stood up. "But I believe that sometimes coincidences aren't coincidences at all. And speaking of, it's no coincidence that we haven't heard a peep from Trevor during this whole conversation. I suspect he's been gaming instead of doing homework. I think there's something going on at school, but it's like pulling teeth to get him to talk."

Alex looked at the business card and thought back to the woman in 2A. There had been something oddly calming about her—maybe it was the way she seemed to genuinely care. And she had an energy about her. Alex couldn't quite put his finger on it. A quiet confidence? Charisma? What was it?

Like someone you'd turn to if you were in trouble?

Yes. That was it exactly.

But there was more to it. He remembered the woman had said she used to be afraid of flying. *She used to be like me*, he thought.

Then, another moment flashed into his mind. What had Raj said during the meeting? Alex tried to replay the conversation in his mind. It was when they had been weighing their options, trying to figure out what to do next. *I am not comfortable with this*, that's what Raj had said. It was the same thing he'd just said to Maggie. He looked down at the crumpled card in his hand. *Chief Discomfort Officer.*

Sometimes, coincidences aren't coincidences.

Without hesitating, he picked up his phone and started typing a message.

FIVE

THE FOREST

Alex's unease grew as he drove farther from the city. His phone's GPS confirmed the route, but still, he hesitated. *Why are we meeting so far outside the city?*

Last night, Andrea (aka the woman in 2A) had replied almost immediately to his text. She said her schedule was full, but she could squeeze him in for a 7:00 a.m. meeting—"sharp," she had added. She didn't give him an address, just dropped a GPS pin with a message: "Follow this. You'll know when you're there." Then one more line: "Wear comfortable shoes and bring a light jacket." That alone had set him on edge.

She seemed so enthusiastic and ready to meet so quickly that Alex wondered if she was trying to sell him something. Maggie was so trusting. It was something Alex loved about her. But he had always been more cautious around people. Was the Brave Sciences Institute some kind of multilevel marketing scheme? A self-help cult? His internal alarm bells were ringing.

Last night, his curiosity—and truth be told, his skepticism—had gotten the better of him. It hadn't taken much searching to find that the Brave Sciences Institute—and its "Chief Discomfort Officer" Dr. Andrea Hastings—seemed legit. Andrea had both an MBA and a PhD in psychology. From what he could tell, she was the real deal. Conference keynotes. Peer-reviewed research. A TEDx talk with over two million views. A best-selling author. At some point, a younger version of Andrea had dedicated her life to exploring the connection between discomfort and life satisfaction.

That sounds like something I need.

The road stretched ahead, mostly empty, lined with trees instead of traffic. It was early, quiet, and disorienting. He was used to heading into the flow—toward the city, toward the buzz. But now he was driving away from all of it. And it unsettled him.

He should be at the office.

Nico had arranged to meet with the board that afternoon to discuss their ideas for winding down the development group over the next six months. Raj and Willow were working on a deck, but Alex had the best handle on the cost and timelines of the prototype.

Yet here he was, heading away from the office to meet a stranger he'd sat next to on a plane.

What am I doing?

For all his research, Alex still had no idea who this woman was. He knew she was confident and calm under pressure—that much was clear from the flight. She was also some kind of expert, clearly. And she'd offered to help.

But does that justify blowing off work in the middle of a crisis?

His head said no. But his gut disagreed.

Something about yesterday's meeting at Keeling didn't sit well. He just couldn't put his finger on what it was.

As Alex pulled into the parking lot, he immediately recognized

Andrea. She stood near a signpost marking a nature preserve, exuding the same quiet confidence she had on the plane. Around her, early morning hikers milled about in small clusters, adjusting gear and studying the large trail map posted on the board.

Interesting place for a meeting.

On impulse, he grabbed a notebook and pen from his backpack. Alex stepped from the car into a stiff breeze. A storm was building. He zipped his jacket as he walked toward Andrea. Even from a distance, he could feel the same sense of warm competence. She seemed completely at ease.

"Thanks for meeting me," he said, shaking her hand.

"Welcome back to ground level," Andrea replied with a warm smile.

Alex looked around. "I feel a little awkward," he said. "To be honest, I'm not sure why I messaged you. It was my wife's idea."

Andrea's smile widened. "I get that a lot." She motioned toward the trail. "Why don't we take a walk?"

Andrea seemed to know where she was headed, and Alex followed her down a marked trail into the forest.

"I wanted to thank you," he said. "For your help on the plane. You really helped me feel a bit more comfortable."

"Are you planning to fly again?"

"Not if I can help it," Alex said, and laughed.

"Then I guess I didn't help," Andrea said. "Not yet, anyway."

Does she always speak in riddles? Once more, Alex wondered if he should be at the office, not wandering in the woods.

As they walked, the path narrowed, and they occasionally stepped aside to let other hikers pass. The wind was calmer, but as

Alex looked toward the treetops, he saw branches swaying wildly in the canopy. Every few moments, an enormous gust would power its way through the leaves, bending even the thickest of the trees.

The storm is really coming on, he thought.

Andrea stopped in the middle of the trail.

"This is it," she said. Then she abruptly turned and walked directly into the dense forest.

Alex stood for a moment.

He scanned the trail. There was no one in sight.

Is this some kind of experiment?

He recalled her unusual job title. *Is she trying to make me uncomfortable? Or something worse?*

No one knew he was here. If something happened, there would be absolutely no way for anyone to find him.

Don't be ridiculous, he scolded himself. *This is a stranger who comforted you on a plane. Does she strike you as some kind of supervillain?*

As if sensing his unease, Andrea called out, "It's not far!"

Alex nodded at another group of passing hikers, then pushed his way into the forest. Andrea led him deeper into the woods, weaving around tree trunks and dodging branches. The forest was becoming even more dense. The trees had grown close together. Less light filtered through the swaying canopy. Above it all, the wind continued to roar.

"This grove was planted by volunteers almost half a century ago," Andrea said over the wind. "This was once pastureland."

"It's beautiful," Alex admitted.

"It is," she agreed. "So. You mentioned some challenges at work?"

Alex took a deep breath, then dove in. He laid it all out—the financial troubles at Keeling, the lack of progress within his team, the board's decision to shut down the division unless they could pull off a Hail Mary, and how the team was now working on a plan to wind things down.

Andrea nodded her head as if in agreement. They walked on, picking their way around tree trunks as the wind grew more intense.

As they moved deeper, the forest began to change.

Alex noticed several trees were leaning. Farther along, entire trunks lay on the ground, their root systems torn from the earth. Andrea stopped and sat on one of the enormous fallen logs. Around them, in a rough circle, trees canted at odd angles. Dead limbs and fallen trunks littered the ground. Sunlight poured into what was almost a clearing. Around them, the wind continued to gust.

Andrea stopped.

"The planters made a mistake," she said. "They were eager to create a beautiful forest, but in some places, they planted the trees too close together. This," she motioned at the clearing of fallen and dying trees, "is the result."

Alex scanned the open area, a stark contrast to the dense forest they had just walked through. "The other trees seem healthy," he said. "Why not these ones? Did they outcompete each other?"

"That's the obvious answer," Andrea said. "But if you could see this forest from the sky, you'd notice that this clearing is almost in the exact center of the woods."

"Did something happen here?"

"Actually," she said pointedly, "you might say it was the exact opposite."

More riddles, he thought.

He looked around the clearing.

"I don't think I understand."

She stood, brushing dirt from her hands.

"This part of the forest is so dense that the trees here were protected from the wind. The problem is that *not enough* happened to them."

Alex looked around again. It made no sense. "Wouldn't the trees on the outside be more susceptible to the wind? They'd take the brunt of a storm."

Andrea smiled, as if she was about to let him in on a secret.

"You would think so, wouldn't you?" She hopped up from the log and turned to face Alex directly.

"In fact, it's the opposite. When trees are exposed to wind, they develop deeper root systems. That helps them survive challenges like drought and high winds. What's more," she continued, "wind carries seeds and pollen farther, and that makes genetically diverse forests that are more resilient to pests and disease."

She raised her arms and turned slowly in a circle. "In short," she said, "the challenge of wind makes a tree grow stronger."

Alex listened to the roar of the wind as it tore through the canopy above. He watched the sway of the enormous branches.

Alex wrote in his notebook:

All growth requires challenge.

It's an intriguing idea, he thought.

He'd have to tell Maggie. She loved this kind of thing. *Sure,* said the voice in his head, *but so what?*

"Um," Alex said. "So—"

Andrea laughed. She seemed delighted by his discomfort.

"You can say what you're thinking," she said.

"I guess I'm wondering what I'm doing here," he admitted.

Andrea smiled. "Imagine these trees in the center of the forest as *people*," she said. "People who are sheltered from the discomfort of challenge or uncertainty."

"Okay?" Alex crossed his arms and stared around the clearing.

"What do you think happens to people when they are able to hide from or avoid discomfort?"

Alex felt as if a small switch had just clicked in his head.

"They become less resilient," he said. "When tough times come, they get knocked down?"

Andrea nodded, smiling. "These trees fell into what I call the *comfort trap*," she said. "They were able to avoid challenge. But instead of keeping them safe, it only made them more vulnerable."

"And this happens to people?"

"It does," Andrea said. "When we avoid discomfort, we take away opportunities to grow, to become strong, and that causes us to become more resilient."

"I'm not sure I follow," Alex said.

"We've come to see discomfort as something *bad*," she replied. "As something to avoid. Nothing could be further from the truth. All discomfort is a form of challenge. And challenge is a requirement for growth. Think of it like a muscle—if you never use it, the muscle weakens."

As if on cue, a powerful gust of wind roared through the canopy overhead. Alex heard an enormous crack and looked up just in time to see a massive tree teetering, its entire root system tearing free from the earth. He stood frozen as the tree crashed to the forest floor, its branches splintering into hundreds of pieces.

He turned to Andrea, his eyes wide.

She nodded as if reading his mind. "Exactly," she said.

Without another word, she turned and walked from the clearing. Alex hesitated for a moment, then followed. His mind churned as they retraced their steps to the trail and headed for the parking lot. In his mind, he saw the tree fall over and over. One minute it seemed strong and resilient; the next it was crashing to the ground.

"So, discomfort is a good thing?" he asked as they reached the main trail. "That feels like the opposite of what we've been told," he said.

"Exactly," Andrea said. "We have come to confuse comfort with happiness. As a result, we've increasingly tried to remove all the discomfort from our lives."

"And that doesn't make us happy?"

"Quite the opposite," Andrea said. "When we remove discomfort, we also remove challenge. Research shows that what really increases our happiness and life satisfaction is embracing challenge, not avoiding it."

"So avoiding discomfort is a trap?"

Andrea stopped and turned to face him.

"Almost everything you really want in life, including happiness, requires growth," she said. "But that growth is always on the other side of something hard. Like the tree, as long as you avoid hard things, you'll remain in the comfort trap. The more you try to avoid discomfort, the tighter the trap becomes."

Alex wrote:

Success and happiness come from embracing challenges.

"So, how do you escape the trap?"

"By not just facing the hard things when they come," she said, "but also *seeking them out*. By becoming, in a word, *brave.*"

The Brave Sciences Institute, Alex thought. He felt a tiny step closer to understanding this mysterious woman.

"It's like getting on a plane," he said, "even though you're afraid of flying."

"Precisely. You might dream of a tropical vacation, for example. But that tropical vacation is on the other side of an uncomfortable flight."

Like Paris, he thought.

"To have that vacation," she said, "you're going to have to be brave."

Alex furrowed his brow. "Before we go any further, I have a question. What's the difference between bravery and courage?"

Andrea nodded, as if she had heard the question before. "Technically, some researchers make a distinction between bravery and courage. But outside of research circles, most people use them interchangeably, and I do too."

"OK." Alex thought back to his terrifying flight. "What if you're not brave?" he asked.

"Ah," Andrea said. "That's the best part. *Anyone* can be brave. You just need to know how."

"I can become brave?"

As the question left his mouth, a crack of thunder rolled across the sky.

"You and anyone else. Studies show that bravery is like a muscle; you can build it over time if you do the work," Andrea said. She eyed the darkening sky. "But brave doesn't mean reckless. Let's head back."

As they walked, Alex found himself turning the idea over in his mind.

Was the comfort trap real? Was it true?

More importantly, he thought, is it true of me?

The closer they got to the parking lot, the more Alex wished he had more time. The idea of the comfort trap made sense, but it also seemed like the doorway to a much deeper conversation. *The comfort trap means something*, he thought. *To me. To my life*. He scribbled as they walked:

Avoiding challenges makes you weaker.

Instead of the sky brightening as they approached the parking lot, the darkness deepened. Alex saw that the sky was a dark, angry gray. The trees were bending wildly in the growing wind, yet they stood strong.

They really are more resilient, he thought.

"If I'm in the comfort trap," he said, "how do I escape? I don't see myself as a courageous person. How do I become braver?"

Andrea nodded. "Excellent question."

She led Alex to a signboard near the trailhead, the same one the other hikers had been studying earlier. Beneath the protective glass cover, a large map detailed the entire preserve. The wind whipped at their clothes, and Andrea had to raise her voice to be heard.

"This is a map of the preserve." She pointed to an area on the sign. "And this is the clearing where we saw the tree fall."

Just as she had said, it was almost exactly in the center of the forest.

"I guess the original tree planters didn't know about the comfort trap," Alex said.

"They would have known that the trees would face challenges," she said. "There will always be storms—both in a forest and in life."

Andrea paused as a powerful gust pushed them back on their heels. She raised her voice to be heard against the growing storm.

"What they didn't realize was how important it was to *seek* challenge," she called. "It's not enough to simply survive storms. You also need to seek out the winds of change if you want to grow. You need a framework for being brave."

Distant thunder rolled. An instant later, a bolt of lightning lit the sky. Before Alex could ask what Andrea meant, the skies opened, and a torrent of rain began to fall.

Andrea laughed. "Run!"

They sprinted for their cars.

SIX

A CHANGE IN PLANS

Alex slid into the car and slammed the door. Rain pelted his windshield in heavy sheets. Gusts of wind rocked the car, swaying it slightly. He yanked off his wet jacket, wiped his face, and exhaled.

He couldn't see Andrea, but he was having a hard time seeing anything through the downpour. His frustration climbed another notch. *I have so many questions.*

He wrote a last idea in his notebook, thankful it stayed dry under his jacket:

> *You escape the comfort trap—and*
> *grow—by becoming brave.*

His phone buzzed in his pocket. He looked at the time and it was already 8:00 a.m.

Nico

Things are looking good. Need your numbers!
Are you getting close?

His unease returned. Were things really looking good?

He thought back to the fallen trees in the clearing. To what Andrea had said. *All growth requires challenge.*

Is this what has been bothering me? Am I behaving like a sheltered tree? The thought followed him as he pulled slowly from the parking lot and onto the wet street.

There was no sign of the mysterious Andrea. Both the rain and the traffic tapered, but Alex barely noticed. His mind was spinning. To all appearances, the tree in the clearing had been just as healthy as any other. It was a vibrant, living thing. But slowly, imperceptibly, it had weakened. Over the months and years, shelter from the challenging winds had left its roots smaller and shallower—until a storm that it should have survived had brought the tree crashing down.

He couldn't get it out of his mind. *Is this really what happens when you don't seek challenges?*

Slowly, a new reality was forming as he reflected on all these months on the development team. The more he'd felt a sense of burnout, the more he'd tried to avoid any kind of adversity. And the worse it had gotten.

But it goes further than that, he thought. *What about Maggie's dream trip to France?*

Alex knew he had been increasingly avoiding it because of his discomfort with flying. But it wasn't just air travel. Day after day, he realized, he found himself just wanting to be home. To spend his evenings in front of a screen. To not think about the challenges of his day.

He gripped the wheel tighter. Am I like the tree? The question hit hard. The answer hit even harder. *I've fallen into the comfort trap.*

Alex used to be *energized* by work. Now he felt drained, powerless. Stuck. Like he wasn't choosing his own path anymore.

He thought of Trevor and Zoey. *What example am I setting for them?*

His phone buzzed again.

Nico

Where are you?

Alex pushed down on the accelerator.

———

He arrived at the office to a team in action. No one even noticed his wet hair and the mud on his shoes.

Raj and Mo were working on the presentation. Willow was conferring with Nico on the other side of the boardroom table. The room felt energized. Nico looked up as Alex entered.

"Alex," he said. "Just in time. Raj and Mo need your numbers for the division shutdown plan."

Mo looked up with his usual grin and waved Alex over. Raj was focused intently on his screen. Alex managed a weak smile and took a seat next to Raj.

Everyone seems so focused, he thought.

Any other morning, he would've been pleasantly delighted to see the team so motivated. *So why does it feel so wrong?*

Alex answered Raj's questions, but his mind was elsewhere. At one point, he looked up to see Willow watching him closely. Is she a mind reader? He turned his eyes away, back to the presentation on the screen. *Willow.* For the first time, Alex connected to the idea that her name was also the name of a *tree*.

He watched Nico and Raj deeply engaged in some part of the pitch. That, too, troubled him. This was the most productive he had ever seen them. *What if we worked this intently on facing challenges instead of running from them?*

His thoughts were interrupted by Raj closing his laptop.

"That's it," Raj said.

"Okay, everyone," Nico said. "We're ready. Thank you all. I'm going to bring this to the board in"—he looked at his watch—"fifteen minutes. With any luck, we'll have the green light for our plans for shutting down the division and reassigning our roles."

Alex scanned the room. Everyone was nodding along. He watched their nodding heads and thought of trees waving in the wind. Before he even realized it, the words were out of his mouth: "Why would we want that?"

"Excuse me?" Nico said, taken aback.

There was a moment of silence as everyone turned to look at Alex.

"Why would we want that?" Alex repeated.

He wasn't sure who was more surprised—him or the rest of the team. They all had the same stunned look on their faces. *What did I just do?* His mind was whirling. Everyone was staring at him, but he had no idea what to say next. All he knew was that something in him had shifted. He wasn't sure he entirely understood Andrea's message, but he understood enough to know that it mattered.

He realized they were waiting for him to speak. But he had no idea what to say. It was Raj who broke the silence. "The alternative is a miracle," he said. "And that's too difficult."

Somewhere in Alex's mind, something shifted.

"What did you say?" he asked Raj.

He saw Raj's eyes widen. "I didn't—"

"No, I mean . . . Can you repeat what you just said?"

Raj looked confused but said hesitantly, "I said it was too hard?"

Alex felt that shifting feeling again, like a puzzle piece falling into place. *Hard.*

What had Andrea said? *Almost everything you really want is on the other side of something challenging.*

Then it hit him. *I'm not the only one in the comfort trap.*

It wasn't just him; it was the whole team. Maybe the whole division. The development team had been at a standstill for months. Was it really that the workload was too much or the challenges too hard? *Or are we trees in the middle of a dense forest, growing weaker?*

"Look," Alex said, "I know you're worried. All of you. I am too. I agree—it's a lot. But doing the easy thing—it doesn't solve our problem." He thought of the tree. "It might even make things worse."

"How could things get any worse?" Raj's voice was rising.

"If we give in to the easy thing," Alex said, "won't we be worse off? Won't the company be even weaker?"

His question was met with silence. Finally, Nico spoke. His gaunt face had grown shinier than ever. "What are you suggesting, Alex?"

Alex opened his mouth, but nothing came out. He realized he had no idea what he was suggesting. All he knew was that they were in the comfort trap. He looked around the room. Raj was flustered, nervous. Mo was wearing his usual grin, but it wasn't reaching his eyes. It was Willow who made the difference. She was looking earnestly at Alex, encouraging him, nodding her head as if to say *go ahead*.

What had Andrea said? About escaping the comfort trap? *You escape by being brave.*

"Alex?" Nico was staring at him.

It's not enough to weather the storm. Sometimes you need to seek the winds of change. Alex took a deep breath and glanced at Willow.

"I suggest we do it," he said. "We find a miracle. A way forward. It might not be easy, but why not try?"

Alex thought he could almost hear Nico's jaw drop. Alex would remember the next few moments as a strange kind of duality. On the one hand, it was pandemonium. Everyone began talking at once. Voices began to rise. Arms were waved. Yet Alex felt a strange sense of peace. It was as if he had just stepped off a high ledge—but had no fear of the fall. It just felt . . . *right.*

"I know what's next," he said. He said it in a low voice, but the room immediately grew quiet. "I mean, I don't know what will happen, but I know what we need to do right now."

Nico stared at him like he was meeting him for the first time. "The board gave us six months to divest and close down," Alex said. "Can you give me one day? If I can't convince you that we should try something different, I'll join you in your plan."

The room was silent. They all looked at each other.

It was Willow who spoke. "I support Alex. It makes sense. We lose nothing by waiting a day, and we might even learn more for our plan."

Raj shook his head and said nothing.

Mo looked around. "I'm happy to go with whatever the group decides," he said.

They all looked to Nico. He was clearly uncomfortable, but Alex saw his narrow face begin to nod. "I will postpone the meeting," he said. "I look forward to what you have to say tomorrow, Alex."

Then he stood up and left the room. The peaceful feeling that had enveloped Alex just moments before evaporated. *What did I just do?*

It was time to reach out to Andrea again. Whatever her mysterious "bravery framework" was, Alex needed it.

He had never felt less courageous.

THE LESSON

**Almost everything you
want is on the other side of hard.**

- All growth requires challenge.

- Success and happiness come from embracing challenges.

- Avoiding challenges makes you weaker.

- You escape the comfort trap—and grow—by becoming brave.

THE
FIRST
DOOR

SEVEN

THE LAB

Alex woke precisely one minute before his alarm, feeling as if his mind had been busy the entire time he slept. He reread Andrea's text from the previous day. It was just as cryptic as her last one:

> Meet me at our office. 7 a.m.
> Brave Sciences Institute—Lab 1.

Lab 1?

The name sounded both scientific and intimidating at the same time.

Andrea's last words echoed in his mind as the storm had forced them into their cars: You need to seek challenges, not just weather them.

Was it true? He was certainly weathering a storm right now. He let the thought go. In a few short hours, he would meet with the team. What was he going to tell them?

An hour later, he arrived at the address.

Alex had expected any one of a hundred medium-sized commercial buildings in the area, but this building was different. It was modern, with a unique mix of wood, steel, and stone construction. He had never seen anything quite like it. And the parking lot was mostly full. *At 7 a.m.!*

A sign marked the building as the Brave Sciences Institute, and based on the flow of people in and out, it seemed more like noon than early morning. As Alex looked for a parking spot, he saw three people heading for the lot. A young man in his twenties, engrossed in his phone. Behind him, an older, well-dressed woman. She was followed by a broad, muscular man with chiseled features.

Were they part of the Brave Sciences Institute?

He checked his phone. It was a few minutes before seven.

Later that morning, his entire team would be gathering at the office. Meanwhile, for the second day in a row, he was meeting a near-stranger in a place he'd never been for a reason he couldn't quite explain.

The urge to turn around and head to Keeling was almost overwhelming.

But then he remembered Andrea's words.

Everything you want is on the other side of something hard.

He took a deep breath, squared his shoulders, and stepped out of the car.

———

Alex wasn't sure what he had expected to find inside.

But it wasn't this.

His first impression was of *light*.

Where the Keeling building was muted, and almost claustrophobic, the Brave Sciences Institute was awash in daylight, and Alex's gaze drifted naturally upward.

He stood in an enormous atrium, three stories high. The vast stretch of the roof was composed almost entirely of glass that scattered the sunlight in every direction, making the room feel both vast and warm at the same time.

In the center of the spacious lobby stood a sleek reception desk. To the left, a wide, elegantly designed staircase with open risers and a polished metal railing ascended to a raised mezzanine—like the upper lobby of a grand conference center. To the right, a matching set of broad steps descended, seamlessly connecting different levels both practically and artistically.

The space was alive with activity. What looked like tour groups stood in sunlit clusters in the lobby, talking excitedly. The twin staircases kept the flow of people moving with purpose, reinforcing this as a place where things happened. Alex could see more groups of people gathered around the railings of the upper lobby, deep in animated conversation.

This is nothing like Keeling, Alex thought.

Alex glanced down. At his feet, an enormous slab of stone was embedded smoothly in the floor. A phrase was chiseled into its surface:

> *It's not because things are difficult that we do not dare,*
> *but because we do not dare that they are difficult.*
> —Seneca[4]

---

4   Seneca, *Moral Letters to Lucilius*, trans. R. M. Gummere (Harvard University Press, 1917).

He stared at the words.

Interesting, he thought.

That seems backward at first. But is it?

Maybe the challenges at Keeling aren't just happening to us.

Maybe we're in a bind because we haven't dared enough in the first place.

A voice pulled him from his thoughts.

"You must be Alex." The receptionist smiled warmly. "Dr. Hastings is expecting you," he said. "Up the stairs to the second level—first double doors on your left. That'll lead you to Lab 1."

As Alex ascended the grand staircase through the vast, sunlit atrium, he scanned the busy space below.

Thriving.

That was the word that came to mind.

At Keeling, it felt like they were merely surviving. It felt different here. It felt refreshing.

This place hummed with energy.

The mysterious Dr. Andrea Hastings was clearly successful. Did the skill of being brave really make the difference?

He reached the top of the staircase, and stepped into the smaller, but no less welcoming, second-floor atrium. Energizing, but unobtrusive, music played in the background, and the groups he had seen from the lower level milled about in conversation.

Alex checked his watch.

He was early, and so he walked a slow circuit of the atrium while he waited. The space was flanked by three sets of stunning double doors. They were enormous, made from a dark, gleaming wood. There was a sign next to each set of double doors: *Lab 1, Lab 2,* and *Lab 3.*

Alex turned in a slow circle, scanning the space.

The rest of the atrium was filled with a tasteful blend of art, photographs, and inspirational quotes. Alex recognized several famous faces in the photos.

Who is *this Dr. Hastings?*

One photograph in particular caught his attention. In it, Alex recognized Andrea. She stood beside a tall man with a crew cut and a stoic bearing. Immediately next to the photo was another that made Alex's stomach do a small somersault. It showed two people in helmets and goggles soaring through the air, arms outstretched. Visible behind them was the open door of a small plane.

Skydiving, Alex thought with a shudder.

Is she crazy?

He moved on to another shot, this one showing Andrea and a well-known actor. Still another captured Andrea with the famous CEO of a large company.

Teaching bravery, it seemed, was big business.

Alex took one last look over the expansive lobby and headed toward the door marked *Lab 1.* As he approached, he could see the rich grain of the wood, inlaid with a quote:

> *Our life is what our thoughts make it.*
> —**Marcus Aurelius**[5]

He glanced at the quote again.

It sounded . . . too simple.

Or maybe a little out there. What have I gotten myself into?

---

5   Marcus Aurelius, *Meditations*, trans. G. Hays (Modern Library, 2003).

Wouldn't it be nice if life worked that way?

He exhaled, reached for the heavy door, and pulled it open.

————

The word *lab* had conjured up visions of scientists in white coats and long benches of bubbling test tubes. Instead, Alex found something that looked every bit like the company gym at Keeling. Cardio equipment, barbells, steel racks—the room was a large, well-equipped gym. Somewhere, he heard the clanking sound of heavy weights.

"Alex, welcome!"

He turned toward the voice and spotted Andrea at the back of the room, stepping off a sleek treadmill tucked beneath a standing desk. He'd heard of desks that adjusted up and down, and even ones with treadmills under them, but he'd never actually seen one in use.

Does this woman ever sit down and relax? he wondered.

"Cool desk," Alex said as she shut her laptop and walked toward him.

"I've never seen one of these in person. I guess it's for people who are serious about keeping their body fit."

She slid her laptop aside and walked toward him with an easy confidence.

Andrea smiled. "I exercise mainly for my brain—but it's good for the body, too. I could fill you in on all the science behind how exercise impacts mood, cognitive function, and peak performance. But since I only have limited time with you today, we'll save that for another day. Right now, I want to hear about you."

She gestured for him to sit, giving him her full attention.

After a brief hello, Alex filled her in on the previous afternoon—how he had realized that they were stuck in the comfort trap and how the team had given him one day to change their minds.

"That sounds like great progress," she said.

"I'm not so sure," he replied. "If anything, I feel *more* trapped. I have just a few hours left, and I don't know what to do."

"How did yesterday feel?" she asked.

"Uncomfortable," he said. "Like I was doing the right thing, but at the same time it felt hard."

"Perfect," Andrea said.

"You said that escaping the comfort trap means being brave," Alex said, "but I'm not sure where to begin. You mentioned some kind of framework?"

Andrea nodded. "Our research has led us to three keys to bravery—a framework we call the Building Bravery Blueprint. Together, they mark a path to higher success, happiness, and life satisfaction."

Alex recalled the three massive doors in the upper lobby. "What are the keys?"

"The first key to developing bravery is *mindset.*"

Alex looked around at the weights and training equipment. "This looks like it's more about the body than the mind," he said. "Why do you call it a *lab*?"

Andrea smiled. "Physical courage doesn't necessarily correlate to emotional courage," she said. "This is just one of the many ways we teach bravery here at the Institute. We also use public speaking, stand-up comedy—anything that pushes people outside of their comfort zone. If it challenges them and makes them uncomfortable, it works."

She smiled at Alex's expression.

"It's true. The methods might seem unconventional, but all of it is based on the best science. The important thing, as you'll see, is that bravery begins with changing how you *think*. Or, as we say here at the lab, developing a *brave mindset*."

Alex took out his notebook and wrote:

To escape the comfort trap, change how you see hard things.

He reread the sentence. Did that make sense?

Wasn't bravery about the things you *did*?

Seeing his expression, Andrea smiled. "You look skeptical."

"I guess I am," Alex said. "I don't think of myself as a courageous person. You saw that firsthand on the plane. I was terrified."

Andrea nodded. "What if I told you I could begin to change your mindset with a single word?"

Alex looked at her.

She laughed again.

"There's that look," she said. "Let's go find out if I'm right."

Alex followed Andrea past the rows of exercise equipment to a fit-looking man—the source, Alex assumed, of all the clanking. As they drew closer, Alex realized it was the man from the photograph in the upper lobby. He was in his mid-sixties. Tall, arrow-straight, and looked as fit as a man half his age.

"This is Jake," she said. "He's a United States Marine Corps veteran, and my right hand here at the lab. He helped me get over my fear of flying. He's going to introduce you to the first key."

Jake gave Alex a firm handshake. "Pleasure," he said.

Alex eyed the intimidating man and smiled back weakly. "I hope you're not expecting much from me. I'm not good at working out."

Jake gave Andrea a quick glance. Alex thought he saw a faint smile pass between them. Alex scanned the equipment and took a deep breath. "Okay," he exhaled. "Where do we start?"

"With language," Jake said.

"Language?" Alex repeated. "I was expecting something more like bicep curls."

"I get that a lot," he said.

Alex couldn't tell if he was joking or not.

"Repeat to me what you said a moment ago," Jake said.

Alex tried to recall. "I'm not good at working out?"

Jake nodded. "Exactly. I'd like you to add one word to that sentence."

"I *suck* at working out?" Alex joked.

"Nice try. The word I want you to use is *yet.*"

Alex thought for a moment. "I'm not good at working out . . . *yet*?"

"Right," Jake said. "Now say it without the question mark."

"I'm not good at working out *yet*."

"Perfect. Now follow me."

That's the word? Alex thought. But he dutifully followed Jake to a metal bar mounted high on the lab wall. Not following Jake didn't seem like an option.

Jake pointed up. "Let's see ten pull-ups."

Alex's jaw dropped. "You're joking."

Jake said nothing.

"I can't," Alex insisted.

He knew this was true. It's not like he'd never worked out. He and Maggie had even gone to a personal trainer together. In the short time they had attended, Alex discovered that he couldn't do more than three pull-ups. After three, he would hang lifeless from the bar, unable to do more than shrug his shoulders.

He realized Jake was staring at him.

"I don't know what to tell you," Alex said. "I *can't*."

Jake continued to stare. He raised his eyebrows.

"Oh," Alex said. "Sure. Got it." *This is nonsense*, he thought. "I can't do ten pull-ups *yet*."

Jake nodded. "Great," he said. "Do one."

Alex looked at the bar. *One? I'm no superhero, but I can definitely do one.*

He reached up to the bar, held tight with both hands, and pulled himself up until his chin was level with the bar. Then he lowered himself down. It wasn't easy—far from it. In fact, he felt almost drained from the effort. But he had done it.

"One more," Jake said.

Alex took a breath. *Might as well get this over with.* He reached up, took hold of the bar again, and did one more pull-up. This one was more difficult. But he managed to get his chin to the bar.

"Excellent form," Jake said.

"Thanks," Alex said. "But that's about my limit. I can't do eight more."

Jake stared at him.

"Okay. I can't do eight more *yet*."

Alex thought his *yet* came out sounding just a little sarcastic.

But at the same time, he felt something inside. It was hard to put his finger on exactly what it was, but saying the word *yet* had made him start . . . *counting*? Was that the right word? Somehow, the word *yet* had made him feel ever so slightly . . . *different*.

"I agree," Jake said. "You can't do eight more *yet*. But judging by your excellent form, I think you could easily do one more. You're not in bad shape, Alex."

Alex knew he probably could do one more. After all, he'd done three before. This was in his range. He reached up and did another pull-up. It wasn't much harder than number two, but not quite as easy as the first one.

"Keep going," Jake said. "Do one more."

Alex surprised himself by pulling himself up yet again. But just barely. He dropped to the ground and looked at Jake. "What just happened? Am I somehow stronger?"

"No," Jake said, and this time he did smile. "That will take some time. The truth is you were always able to do four pull-ups. You just never got there before."

"And somehow saying *yet* helped?"

"The first lesson of yet is that it transforms impossibility into possibility," Jake said.

"What do you mean?"

"What do you think would have happened if I hadn't prompted you to say *yet*?" Jake asked.

Alex considered this. "I never would have done even one."

"Exactly. *Yet* made it possible to *start*. It created a sense of possibility, however small, instead of closing down the conversation entirely."

It was hard to argue the point. If Jake hadn't prompted him, Alex was pretty sure he'd be out in the parking lot by now.

"Still, that doesn't change the fact that I can't do ten pull-ups."

Jake raised his eyebrows again and smiled.

"*Yet*," Alex said, and found himself smiling along.

Jake looked up at the bar. "What do you think about another one?"

To his surprise, Alex realized that taking a small break had allowed his arms to rest just a little. "I think I could do one more," he said. *Did I just say that?*

Jake nodded, and Alex, to his delight, managed to pull himself up one more time. It was slow and awkward, but he did it.

"That's five! Keep going," Jake said.

This time, Alex managed to pull himself halfway before his arms gave out. He kicked his legs, as if he could somehow swim his way to the bar, but it was no use. He dropped back to the floor.

"I can't," he said, breathing heavily.

Jake cleared his throat with a dramatic *ahem*.

"I can't *yet*," Alex said.

For the next few minutes, Alex and Jake performed what seemed to Alex like a kind of dance. Alex would rest briefly, and Jake would encourage him to try again. Each time Alex was discouraged, Jake would remind him to use the word *yet*. Eventually, he managed to do two more pull-ups. That was seven! But his arms were growing heavy. He reached up, grabbed the bar, and tried again. He struggled up a few inches, his legs kicking in vain, then dropped to the floor.

"I can't," he said—then added *yet* before Jake could speak. The ex-Marine nodded and pointed at a sign on the wall that read *Don't Quit Until You're Proud.*

"How do you feel?" Jake said.

I do feel proud, Alex thought. "Spent," he laughed. "I'd punch you if I could actually lift my arms."

Jake chuckled. "Did you just set a personal record for pull-ups?"

Alex felt an unexpected swell of pride. "I did," he said.

"Do you think you could, at some point, do ten?"

Alex was about to blurt out *no* but caught himself. *Ten is only three more. That's not much.*

"Hmm. Maybe not yet, but I'm sure I could do it if I keep training."

Jake stared at him.

"What?" Alex said.

"Did you hear what you just said?"

The realization hit him, and he laughed. "The power of *yet*," Alex said.

Jake patted him on the back. "Welcome to the brave mindset," he said.

His arms limp but his spirit soaring, Alex headed back to where Andrea stood at the other end of the room.

EIGHT

THE BRAVE MINDSET

Andrea motioned for Alex to take a seat in a recovery area with benches and watercoolers. She sat down across from him.

"What just happened?" Alex asked.

"Do you remember yesterday when I told you that we have misinterpreted discomfort?"

"Yes," Alex said. "It's led us to the comfort trap."

"Precisely. We think challenges reduce our happiness and well-being, when in fact, it's the opposite."

"So how do I become brave?"

"It starts with understanding that we have also misunderstood the word itself," Andrea said. "We think of courage as only being about action. If you do brave things, you're a brave person."

"Isn't that true?"

"You certainly need action," Andrea said, "but that's not where bravery begins. Being brave begins with how we think. It begins with activating the brave mindset."

"I think I just experienced it, but . . . what exactly is the brave mindset?"

"You remember the comfort trap," Andrea said.

"We get stuck when we start to see discomfort as a bad thing," Alex said.

"Exactly. So our first step out of the trap is to change how we see the things that challenge us. We call this new way of seeing challenge the brave mindset."

Alex frowned. "What exactly is the new way of seeing things?"

"The brave mindset teaches us that challenges are not obstacles—they're opportunities for growth. Think of it like lifting weights: The resistance is what makes your muscles stronger. The same is true for life. The hardest moments shape us into something better. They make you stronger."

She continued. "Research shows that if you believe stress and challenges are harmful for you, they will be. Your body and mind will respond negatively, making it harder to push through. But if you believe stress and challenges are good for you—if you see them as fuel for growth—your body and mind will adapt. You'll be more optimistic, more resilient, and more likely to succeed."

She leaned forward slightly. "Stress and adversity aren't going away. The key isn't avoiding them—it's learning to respond in a way that makes you stronger. It all starts with mindset. Challenges are not here to break you; they are here to build you."

Alex thought about his experience at the pull-up bar. His arms ached now, and he knew they would feel worse tomorrow. But he also knew that the pain was a sign that his muscles were going to grow stronger.

He wrote:

Challenges don't diminish you;
they strengthen you.

"That makes sense," he said. "But I'm still not quite clear on how the word *yet* helped me do more pull-ups. I mean, I know it did. But I don't understand how."

"*Yet* is a doorway to the brave mindset," Andrea said. "It's like a trip wire to trigger a new way of thinking."

"Jake told me that it helps create hope," Alex said.

"He's right. One of the challenges of the comfort trap," Andrea said, "is that it narrows your future. The first job of the brave mindset is to open up to possibility instead. We do that using the word *yet.*"

"So when I use *yet* . . . I feel optimistic?"

"The most important shift of using *yet* is to put you in what we call a *growth mindset.* Instead of believing your abilities are fixed, you start to see them as things you can develop with effort, learning, and persistence. That way, you begin to view adversity, setbacks, and failure not as roadblocks but as part of the process of growth."

"That makes sense. But . . . one word does all that?"

"No—you do that. But *yet* is the activating ingredient. It's like the yeast that helps the bread rise."

Alex wrote:

*The word **yet** can activate the brave mindset.*

"You may not realize it," Andrea said, "but inside your mind there is an ongoing dialogue. We call it self-talk."

"I'm quite familiar with that," Alex said ruefully.

Andrea looked at his expression. "It sounds like I don't need to tell you that self-talk can be helpful or harmful," she said.

Alex nodded in agreement.

"If your son said he was bad at math, what would you tell him?"

"That he wasn't bad at math, he just hadn't learned it *yet*." Alex smiled as the word came out of his mouth.

Andrea nodded. "Exactly. The problem is, we don't always extend the same grace to ourselves. Instead of talking to ourselves, we just listen—to doubts, fears, and old beliefs that hold us back. But here's the thing: What we tell ourselves matters. If we want to cultivate bravery, we must take control of that dialogue. We need to talk to ourselves in a way that moves us forward. That's why a simple word like *yet* can be so powerful—it helps us take control of our inner dialogue and direct our thoughts from what we can't do to what is possible."

Alex looked at Andrea, still puzzled. "It seems like such a small change."

"Small but powerful," Andrea said. "Look at it this way. When you started with Jake, you saw ten pull-ups as impossible."

"That's true," Alex said.

"Were you intimidated?"

"Absolutely."

"Was it hard?" Andrea asked.

"I can barely move my arms," Alex said.

"Did you do ten pull-ups?" Andrea asked.

"No."

"And how do you feel?"

The answer came out of Alex's mouth almost before he had time to think. "I feel fantastic."

Andrea nodded. "So you tackled a seemingly impossible, intimidating task, struggled painfully, and then failed? Is that an accurate summary?"

Alex opened his mouth, but no sound came out.

"And yet you feel fantastic and are confident you can do ten soon."

"I don't understand," Alex said.

"Ah," Andrea said, "you don't understand—"

"*Yet*," Alex said before she could finish.

Alex flexed his arms. He could feel them stiffening from the pull-ups.

"So I failed at the task, technically. I struggled and it really hurt at times. But I feel confident and almost *excited* about trying it again? How can that be?"

Andrea nodded at the question. "Most people believe that happiness comes *after* success," she said. "But all of our research here at the institute is clear: Happiness—positive emotions like joy, love, gratitude, and awe—is not the result of success. It is the fuel that drives it."

She let that sink in before continuing.

"All this time, the world has been looking at it backward. When you generate a brave mindset each day, you equip yourself to perform at your best and succeed. You take on challenges, persist through setbacks, and ultimately succeed. Happiness doesn't come from success," she said. "It's one of the things that creates it."

Alex jotted down her words as Andrea walked him to the door of the lab:

> *Happiness doesn't come from success;*
> *it helps create success.*

"*Yet* taps into a way of seeing the world," Andrea continued, "like a lens to help you look at challenges differently. When you said *yet*, you set in motion a series of shifts in your thinking about hard things."

"What shifts?" Alex asked.

"*Yet* says that the challenge you are facing is temporary, not permanent," Andrea said. "You might not be good at working out now, but one day, you could be. In that context, *yet* opens the door to a positive future."

"It's more hopeful?"

"Exactly!" Andrea said. "And that hope means more than you think. Once we start to believe that we could be good at working out, we start to wonder how."

Alex realized this was true. "I was just thinking that if I did this three or four times each week, I would probably be a lot stronger."

"*Yet* is the gateway to *how*," Andrea said. "We need action, but we have to think differently first. The brave mindset is about shifting from avoiding hard things to embracing them."

The light bulb came on for Alex. "And that gets me out of the comfort trap!"

Andrea beamed. "*Yet* is the doorway to the brave mindset. Anytime you feel like your mind might be holding you back, start with the word *yet*. That word is the entry point to bravery in all the areas of your life. From tough conversations to career risks to trying new things."

Alex considered all of this. The truth was, he did feel differently about working out now. He was still a little intimidated, to be sure. And he wouldn't call himself strong.

Yet, he thought. *Yet. That's right.* He wasn't strong *yet*. But he could be. And he could make that happen. Andrea opened the door to the lab, and Alex looked out into the soaring space of the atrium.

I've got to face the team, he realized. *And pull-ups aren't the same as saving jobs.* He turned back to Andrea.

"I understand that being brave starts with how you think," Alex said. "But I've got a room full of people to deal with now, and I don't know what to do."

"Do you remember our meeting on the plane?" Andrea asked.

"I wish the answer was no," Alex said. "I try to forget those flights."

"I told you that I used to be afraid of flying," she said.

Alex still found it hard to believe. Andrea seemed so confident, so sure of herself, that he had trouble imagining that she had ever been afraid of anything.

She seemed to read his thoughts. "It's true. And I'm not just talking about a little discomfort. I'm talking full-blown panic attacks."

"It's hard to believe," Alex said. "You were the one comforting me on the flight."

"I've come a long way," Andrea said and smiled, "but I can tell you where that journey began. It began with *yet*. I changed my language. I used to say, 'I'm not comfortable flying.' That was a euphemism—the truth was, I was terrified. But I changed my language to 'I am not comfortable flying *yet.*'"

"And that fixed it?"

Andrea laughed. "Not at all. But that was the turning point. It shifted my thinking. I began to see my fear of flying as something I could work on. It wasn't permanent. It was a place I could grow. Flying was a challenge, nothing more."

Alex considered this. "I understand that intellectually," he said, "but what did you do next?"

"I decided right there that instead of trying to escape every potential flight—either before or during—I would try to embrace the challenge of every flight."

"You were starting to escape the comfort trap," Alex said.

"Before that," Andrea said, "I had been making the same fundamental mistake over and over. Instead of trying to escape the trap, I was trying to avoid the challenge of flying altogether. That just made the trap tighter. Once I started to think of bravery as a muscle, I realized I could practice it. I could work out my brain! So I began by changing how I thought about flying. Every day."

Alex imagined himself going back to the airport. Just the thought made him nervous. "What did you actually do on your next flight?"

"Ah," Andrea said. "That's a conversation for another time."

"I'm not sure how much time I have," Alex protested. "I need a miracle, not another conversation."

Andrea nodded. "I hear you. But sometimes what we think is a miracle is really just bravery in action."

Alex let out a breath. "Action sounds good. What do I need to do?"

"Bravery begins with how you think, Alex," Andrea said firmly. "Let's start with that."

She opened the door a little wider.

"What we focus on," Andrea said, "is what we become. Neurobiology has taught us that the brain changes based on our thoughts. The brave mindset is about changing our thinking—shifting from negative, or pessimistic thoughts, to positive, optimistic ones."

"That makes sense," Alex said. "But I can't help but wish you'd just tell me what to do."

Andrea smiled. "I am, Alex," she said. "I am."

He stared at the door, reluctant to leave.

"One more thing," he said. "What's behind the other two doors?"

"Come back tomorrow," Andrea said, "and you'll find out."

Always more mysteries, Alex thought.

As Alex walked out of Lab 1, he remembered the quote he saw on his way in. He stopped to reread it. "Our life is what our thoughts make it." It was starting to make sense.

He opened his notebook and jotted down his key takeaway in his own words:

Your thoughts shape who you become.

His phone buzzed. It was Nico.

It was time to face the team.

NINE

THE PITCH

Alex left the lab with mixed feelings. Andrea had given him so much hope. It all made so much sense. If she was right, then it was possible he could develop a brave mindset the same way he could build muscle. Challenges, it seemed, were like heavy weights in a gym—they could be daunting (*even painful*, he thought, as an ache shot through his tired arms), but if you saw them as things that helped you get stronger, you . . . well, you eventually got stronger. He thought of Andrea and her own fear of flying. If anything, it seemed like she might have been more afraid of flying than he was. Was it possible that he could become comfortable flying? Could he even take Maggie to Paris one day?

The thought made him feel uncomfortable. He wasn't sure he could do it.

Yet, he reminded himself. *Yet.*

The farther he drove from the Brave Sciences Institute, however, the less confident he began to feel. What was he going to say when he arrived?

Being brave is a habit. Andrea's words came back to him. *You get to decide whether challenges are something to avoid or something to embrace.*

"Okay," he said aloud. "What do I know?"

The team is stuck in the comfort trap.

"What do you do when you're in a trap?"

You try to escape.

That was it. They were trying to escape the wrong thing. Instead of escaping the comfort trap, they were trying to escape the challenge. And that was making the trap tighter. It was like flying, he realized. He spent so much energy trying to avoid flying instead of thinking of flying as something he might get better at. *I need to help them escape the trap, not the challenge.*

Somehow, he was going to have to point the team toward discomfort. But how? He called Maggie as he drove toward Keeling.

"Tell me something good," she said. "I've got a roomful of students who won't budge an inch today."

"Not *yet*," Alex said. "But it's early—and you will. You'll find a way."

There was a pause. "Well, that's an optimistic spin, Mr. Not Yet," she laughed. "Thank you."

Alex realized the words he had used and laughed along. He caught Maggie up as he described his unexpected morning at the Brave Sciences Institute and the idea of escaping the comfort trap by using the word *yet*.

There was another pause. Alex could almost hear her thinking.

"That might be the perfect way to get these kids going," she said. "Thanks for the tip! Gotta run."

———

As Alex parked in the employee lot and looked to where the Keeling office stood, he felt an urge to just drive away.

To escape, he thought. *Everything you want is on the other side of something hard.*

"Nope," he said aloud. "Not today."

Then he stepped out of the car and headed to meet the team.

Alex found a very different boardroom awaiting him. The previous day, he had arrived to a hive of activity. Everyone had been engaged in preparing the pitch, the team oriented around a common goal. Today, he walked into silence.

The entire team was there. Mo. Raj. Willow. And Nico, sitting at the head of the table. All heads turned to look at him. He walked across the room and sat down.

"Alex," Nico said. "Right on time."

Alex took a deep breath. *I'm uncomfortable,* he thought. *But maybe that's okay.* No one spoke.

"As I said yesterday," Alex began, "I think we should consider the fact that the board might be wrong. Maybe we can find a solution. I think we should try to make the division profitable. I don't think the board really wants to close the division. I think they probably just feel like they have no choice . . . unless something changes."

No one spoke. But he saw Raj shake his head in disappointment. Mo seemed to be staring anywhere but at Alex. Alex snuck a glance at Willow, who met his eyes but looked concerned.

"We don't even have a prototype," Mo said.

"We don't even have vendors and costing," Raj said.

They're in the comfort trap, Alex thought. *They're like sheltered trees, and now they're facing a storm. How do I get them to embrace discomfort?*

Alex wished he could call Andrea. She'd know what to do.

But you're on your own. You need to be brave. He looked around the room. Raj had just tossed his pen angrily on the table. Mo was wide-eyed. In response to Alex's silence, Willow and Nico were back to quietly discussing the pitch to the board.

It was all unraveling. Alex's stomach tightened, much like it had on the plane. He squirmed in his seat and another ache shot through his back and shoulders. *Ouch.* Those pull-ups. The pull-ups. He had done seven pull-ups! He still couldn't quite believe it. *How did I do that?*

"Yet," Alex murmured. The room quieted.

"Alex?" Nico said.

"*Yet,*" Alex said. "We don't have a prototype *yet.* We don't have all the information *yet.*"

"Same same," Raj said. "We don't have it. Period."

Alex nodded at him, then repeated, "We don't have it *yet.*"

Raj raised his hands in frustration. Alex turned to Nico. "I know it's a small thing," Alex said, "but bear with me."

Yet *opens the door to* how, Alex thought.

"If we don't have the prototype yet," Alex said, "that does assume we'll *eventually* have it."

Mo said, "But not in time for—"

This time, it was Nico who interrupted. He seemed thoughtful. "Let's let Alex finish."

"Tell me this," Alex said. "Is it possible to eventually finish the prototype?"

"Of course," Raj said dismissively. The other heads nodded.

"Then we all agree we don't have it yet," Alex said. "That means it's coming. But when is that?"

The room was silent. Nico nodded. "Point taken, Alex. We don't actually know . . ." he paused, then added, "*yet*."

"Then," Alex said, "how are we so sure we can't do it?"

Alex let the thought linger, then added gently, "Imagine how we'd feel if we knew it was possible, but didn't even try."

———

Something had shifted.

Just as it had at the pull-up bar, the word *yet* seemed to have unlocked a different way of thinking. It was just as Andrea had said—it was a doorway to a new mindset. The word *yet* had changed the conversation. It was subtle, but it was real.

The team was still far from unified. Raj and Mo, in particular, seemed more mired in the comfort trap than the others. And almost immediately, Alex realized they were falling back into old patterns. But Nico, to his credit, kept steering them back. Of anyone, he seemed to be the most willing to embrace the idea. When they found themselves circling the same old drain—an endless conversation about costs on one area of the prototype—Willow said, "We don't know." Nico stood up and walked to a whiteboard in the corner. He wrote **YET** in large black letters, then returned to his seat.

"Right," Willow said and giggled a little. "Yet."

Slowly—very slowly—they made progress.

There was a moment where Alex knew it all hung in the balance. Raj was digging in his heels, insisting they couldn't do it. Mo, who tended to side with Raj to keep the peace, was doing the same, albeit cheerfully.

Willow also seemed to be struggling. "I don't understand what we're trying to accomplish," she said. "We keep coming back to this word *yet*, and we're trying to support you, Alex. But we're not actually doing anything."

She's not entirely wrong, Alex thought.

He tried to replay the conversation with Andrea at the lab. There was something. What had she said?

There's a similar error with being brave . . .

Alex realized his mistake. *Being brave begins with how we think.*

"I hear you, Willow," he said. "It does feel like we aren't actually doing anything. But we've been stuck for months. Maybe we need to change the way we think first."

To his surprise, she nodded. Alex thought back to his morning at the lab and how Jake had asked him to do ten pull-ups. Alex had practically laughed in his face. And yet, here he was, just hours later, having done seven pull-ups and knowing—knowing without a doubt—that doing ten was now possible. All that in such a short time.

"Here's what I propose," Alex began. "If we can all agree on one thing—one thing that will help us move forward—will you give me one more day?"

Willow spoke up. "I'd like to be supportive," she said, "but I think I have to ask at this point: What are you going to do with one more day?"

Alex looked around the room and then back at Willow. "I'm going to come back with a plan."

Raj snorted. But Nico raised his hand. "And what if we don't agree with your plan?"

"Then you go back to the board's shutdown plan, and we're done. I will fully support you."

Nico looked around the room. One by one, each person nodded. Nico finished his circuit with Raj, who finally dropped his pen in frustration and said, "Fine."

"We are in agreement," Nico said.

"Hold on," Willow said. "There was an *if* there: if we all agree on one thing. What's the one thing?"

Alex nodded. "Well, we've already agreed that we don't have a prototype *yet*," he said. He could almost hear Raj roll his eyes. "My question is this: Is it possible for the people in this room to create one?"

The question was met with silence.

"Of course it is," Willow said.

Alex looked around the room. Everyone, even Raj, seemed to agree. It was possible. Alex looked at Nico.

"Well, Alex," he said, "it looks like you've got your day."

The meeting ended, and one by one, the team members began to file out of the room.

"Stay a minute, Alex?" It was Nico.

Uh-oh, Alex thought.

"I want to tell you—I'm glad we did this today," Nico said. "No matter how things turn out, today changed the way I see things. You've taught me something about how to approach challenging situations. I appreciate that. If we can pull this off, it would be a one hell of a win."

Alex nodded.

"But let me be clear. You can't just ask for one more day forever. That approach ends here. I will meet with the board the day after tomorrow. There will be no more extra days. Tomorrow, we make a decision as a team, and we present to the board the following morning."

Nico stood and left the room.

Alex sat alone for a very long time.

THE LESSON

Bravery begins with how you think.

- To escape the comfort trap, change how you see hard things.

- Challenges don't diminish you; they strengthen you.

- The word **yet** can activate the brave mindset.

- Happiness doesn't come from success; it helps create success.

- Your thoughts shape who you become.

THE
SECOND
DOOR

TEN

THE SAME BOAT

Alex walked back to his office, uncertain whether he'd just won a victory or a stay of execution. Nico's warning shot had landed. By tomorrow, they would either be telling the board they couldn't complete the prototype, or they'd need to—

Need to what, exactly? He didn't know. But that felt somehow okay. He'd been trying to share his ideas for months but had felt stifled. *Now you're getting your shot,* he thought. *Maybe all it took was a brave mindset.*

He had just reached his desk when there was a knock at the door. He looked up to see Willow leaning against the doorframe, her arms folded, staring at him.

"What?"

Willow cocked her head to one side. "You're different," she said.

Now it was Alex's turn to stare. "What do you mean?"

"I don't know," she said. "But you don't seem like you."

"What does—"

"No. I take that back," she said. "I think you seem *more* like you."

"Is that a good thing?"

Willow laughed. "That's definitely a good thing," she said.

She stood, continuing to appraise him.

"Can I—help with something?" Alex asked.

Willow smiled. "Nope! I just wanted to say whatever you're doing, keep doing it." And then she was gone.

Alex stared at the empty doorway. Was he different? He didn't feel different. Well, his arms hurt. There was that.

But that's not all, is it? No. It wasn't. Something had changed. Inside Alex was a tiny, flickering sense of something he hadn't felt in a long time.

It was, he realized, *pride. And it felt great.*

He felt the pain in his arms. He thought of how, just a day ago, the team had been willing to give up. Even if it ended here, they had accomplished something. Being brave really did start with how you think. And now that he'd started to think more bravely, Alex knew he didn't want the story with Keeling to end here. But what came next? Nico had been clear: no more delays. But it was Willow's comment that was troubling Alex now: *We're not doing anything.*

It was true in some meaningful way. Just *thinking* wasn't going to save Keeling and its employees. They had to act. The small flickering of pride seemed to snuff out. Alex had no idea what to do next.

But he knew who did.

———

This time, Alex wasn't surprised when Andrea suggested they meet early the following morning at the Brave Sciences Institute. And there was no map in her message—they seemed to have settled into an unspoken rhythm.

What was surprising was his peace of mind. He found himself daydreaming on the commute home—as if he didn't have a care in the world. As if his company wasn't in deep trouble and the fate of the world didn't seem to be resting on him.

A honk startled him back to reality. The light had turned green. *Where was I just now?*

Alex realized he had been thinking about flying. He had been imagining him and Maggie on a flight. A *flight*, of all things. They were on their way to Paris. They clinked glasses of champagne in first class. They were so happy.

That was—well, that was crazy, wasn't it? Alex hadn't been able to even touch his drink on his last flight. The idea that he would be cheerfully clinking champagne flutes on a plane was ridiculous.

And yet, somehow, it wasn't.

His fear was by no means gone. That week, Trevor had showed him an extreme sports video of a man in a wingsuit jumping from a cliff, and Alex's heart had climbed halfway out of his chest as he waited anxiously for the parachute to open. Even now, having left his daydream, he could feel an anxious flutter in his stomach just at the thought of being trapped in a plane. But the flutter seemed different. Instead of something to avoid, it felt like a sign of something important. Better yet, it seemed like something he could work on.

Something is happening, Alex thought. *Something good.* The feeling of wonder lasted all the way home, right up to the moment he opened the front door.

"Hello!" Alex called out as he opened the door. "Hey, do you want to go for dinner at—"

He broke off.

Maggie stood in the hallway, her hands on her hips. She was staring up the stairs toward the bedrooms on the second floor.

"What's going on?"

"It's Trevor. His teacher called. Apparently, he's been spending recess and lunchtime in the classroom instead of going out with the rest of the kids. He won't tell me why."

Alex's heart sank. "I'll check on him," he said.

Alex knocked softly and pushed open Trevor's bedroom door. The ten-year-old was lying on his bed, immersed in a video game.

Alex crossed the room and sat down beside him. Neither of them spoke. He wasn't sure how to begin. Trevor had been struggling. He was a small kid, drawn more to computers and books than to sports. Alex was pretty sure he was intimidated by the games at recess. And truth be told, Alex could sympathize. He'd never been much of an athlete himself. His experience with the pull-ups had been a reminder.

Alex interrupted the thought. His experience at the Brave Sciences Institute had taught him that he wasn't an athlete *yet*. Who said he couldn't become one if he wanted?

Yet.

Alex leaned in to watch Trevor play. "You're getting pretty good at this," he said.

Trevor shrugged, and Alex watched him pull off a complicated series of maneuvers. *I think he might be showing off for me.* Alex smiled.

"Let me ask you something," Alex said.

Trevor paused the game and looked up at Alex. *He looks so sad,* Alex thought.

"Do you remember when you got that game for Christmas?"

Trevor nodded.

"We played it together," Alex said.

"You were really bad," Trevor said. Alex thought he saw a trace of a smile.

"Hey, mister," Alex said. "You were pretty bad yourself."

At that, Trevor laughed. "You're right," he said. "I was pretty terrible. I couldn't even get past the first level."

"What do you think happened?" Alex said.

Trevor cocked his head. "I don't know," he shrugged. "I just kept playing until I could do it."

"Why didn't you give up?" Alex asked.

Trevor's eyes narrowed, and he turned to face Alex on the bed. "Is this one of those times where we're talking about something, but really we're talking about something else?"

Alex couldn't help it. He laughed out loud.

"Guilty," Alex said. "You are getting too smart for your own good."

Trevor grinned, pleased with himself.

"I hear you've been skipping recess," Alex said.

"The kids always play soccer," Trevor said, "and I suck at it."

Alex thought back to his experience at the lab. *It's like I'm listening to myself speak,* he thought.

"I learned something at work today," Alex said. "Like a magic word."

"Really?"

"I had to do something that was hard, and I didn't think I was very good at it. What I wanted to do was quit. Instead, I learned to use the magic word—*yet*. I told myself I wasn't good at it *yet*. But if I practiced, I could get better."

Trevor was silent. "Like the video game," he said after a pause. "I knew I wasn't good at it yet. But if I just kept trying, eventually I'd do it."

I love this kid, Alex thought. "Exactly," he said. "Maybe recess is a little bit like your video game."

Trevor cocked his head again, considering. "Maybe," he said. Then he picked up his controller, and Alex decided that was enough of a lecture for one night.

He tousled Trevor's hair and headed for the door. He was about to close it behind him when he heard Trevor say, "Is dinner ready . . ."

There was a long pause.

"Yet?" he finished.

He didn't look up from his game, but Alex could see him grinning.

How about that? Alex thought. *Maybe they do listen.*

ELEVEN

TAKING THE PLUNGE

By the time he arrived at the Brave Sciences Institute the following morning, the dull ache in Alex's arms from his pull-up experience had been replaced by something far more intense. Just reaching for and lifting his coffee cup made his back and bicep muscles scream out.

If this is what being brave feels like, he thought, *I'm not sure I want to become any more courageous.*

Yet, there was something satisfying about the discomfort. For all the pain, Alex knew that he'd probably be able to do an extra pull-up in a week or two. He was growing, getting stronger.

Just twenty-four hours earlier, he had been telling Jake he wasn't good at working out. Now, he was surprised to find he was looking for another chance to test himself.

Bravery begins with how you think, he thought. *I'm escaping the comfort trap.*

Alex reflected on his sense of pride after his meeting. He thought of his growing confidence that he could do more pull-ups. That he could get better. He didn't feel like an athlete. And he still felt wildly out of his depth in the situation at Keeling. But he also felt like he was growing. He was becoming.

What had Willow said? *You're different.*

I think I am.

Just as quickly as the thought came, it was replaced by another: *Now what?* Suddenly, his daydream from the day before seemed as distant as Paris itself. The clock was ticking at Keeling. He had to figure this out. Not for the first time, he thought of Carter. Caffeinate and think it through. But how much coffee could one person drink? What Alex really wished was that he could think it through with Carter. He would know what to do.

Not going to happen, he thought. *You're on your own.*

Alex entered the impressive atrium of the Institute. Near the main desk, he saw Andrea speaking to a group. As he walked closer, he saw they all wore badges marked Visitor. Andrea caught his eye and smiled as she wrapped up her presentation.

"Alex," she said. "I'm so glad that you're back."

Alex watched as the group dispersed through the sunlit lobby.

"All of this to help people become brave?" Alex asked, motioning at the soaring ceilings.

Andrea nodded. "Every company, every team, and every individual can benefit from becoming braver," she said. "When I'm not traveling to teach the keys to bravery, I try to meet with the tour groups in person. I speak at schools pro bono, and the kids also like to come visit."

"You must fly a lot," Alex said. "I still don't know how you manage it."

"Then you're in the right place for answers," Andrea said. "Let's head upstairs."

Alex followed Andrea up the grand stairs to the second-floor atrium. She led him to the second set of stunning wooden doors, marked *Lab 2*.

The second key, Alex thought. Like the first door, this one was engraved with a quote:

> *How long are you going to wait before*
> *you demand the best of yourself?*
> **—Epictetus**[6]

Simple, yet profound. Alex traced the engraving with his fingertips, the weight of the words settling in. "These doors are beautiful," he said.

"And symbolic," Andrea answered. "Remember the nature preserve we visited? I arranged to purchase the logs from any fallen trees that blocked the trails. We had a master carpenter create these beautiful doors and helped the nature preserve at the same time."

She pushed the heavy doors open on silent hinges. Alex looked at the carved text. Was he demanding the best of himself? The honest answer was no. So how long was he going to wait? He read the quote once more, then followed Andrea into the lab.

Yesterday's doors had led into a large, open space that was more or less a gym. This room was a similar size, but the lighting was dim, and Alex thought he heard the sound of flowing water. A raised

---

6   Epictetus, *The Enchiridion*, trans. R. Dobbin (Penguin Books, 2008).

platform ran the length of the room, holding a series of large boxes. Each was the size of a refrigerator, with pipes leading in and out. Andrea pointed to a desk, and they sat down.

"How are you feeling?" A mischievous smile touched her lips.

"If you're asking about my arms," Alex said, "I can barely move them."

She laughed. "How did it go at work?"

Alex recapped the meeting, telling Andrea how using the word *yet* had helped open the team to a more positive future. How it seemed to have led them—at least partially—out of the comfort trap.

"I have to admit," he said, "I never would have believed it if I hadn't seen it myself."

Andrea nodded, pleased.

"But," he added, "the team is pressuring me for action. I don't know what to do next."

"Of course," Andrea said. "Bravery isn't just something you think about—it's something you do. A brave mindset is important because it helps us take action. But mindset alone isn't enough. We can't stop there.

"A brave mindset helps you see opportunities, but only brave action allows you to seize them. If we stop at mindset, we get stuck in the dreamer state."

She tilted her head. "Have you ever met someone who talks endlessly about their big dreams and aspirations but never takes a single step toward making them happen?"

Alex had—too many times. In fact, if he was being honest, he'd been that person before—full of ideas, but not being brave enough to act.

She didn't wait for an answer. "Some people teach that if you just visualize success, it will magically come true. That's simply not true. It's not backed by science. Vision boards and belief alone don't create results—action does. Bravery means stepping forward, even when it's uncomfortable. You have to take bold action to turn possibility into reality."

Alex made a note:

Brave action turns potential into reality.

"So the second key in the building bravery framework is action?"

"Exactly," Andrea said. "A brave mindset is only the start. You also need to take what we call that *brave action*."

"Is that different from—well, regular action?"

Andrea laughed. "It is very different. Regular action doesn't require bravery—it is easy. It is going through the motions, checking off tasks without real growth or meaning. This can lead to boredom and complacency. Brave action means stepping forward even when you're afraid. You don't wait until the fear disappears; you move through discomfort because you know it's the right thing to do. It starts by setting challenging goals, not just any goals. Brave goals stretch you. Brave goals should scare you a little, in the best possible way. If it doesn't make you a little nervous, it's probably not brave enough."

Alex wrote:

Brave goals challenge you—if it is easy, it's not brave.

"Brave goals challenge you," Andrea continued, "but they also are meaningful. They matter."

"Why is that important?"

"If your goal isn't meaningful to you," she said, "then you won't rise to the challenges that come with it. And you can be sure there will be challenges."

Alex frowned. "I thought goals were supposed to be SMART?"

Andrea raised an eyebrow.

Alex straightened a little, pleased that he actually remembered this. "You know—specific, measurable, achievable, relevant, and time-bound." He leaned back, crossing his arms, impressed he remembered the acronym.

Andrea grinned. "Nice work. And there's nothing wrong with making brave goals SMART. But SMART goals miss the two most important elements—*challenging* and *meaningful*. If your goal isn't truly meaningful to you, you won't push through when things get tough. And if it's not challenging, it won't push you to grow."

She set down her notepad. "Once you have a brave goal written down, you need to plan how to reach it in clear, achievable steps. Like climbing a ladder—one rung at a time."

Alex exhaled. "To be honest, I've tried that. I know about writing goals and developing plans to achieve them. But somehow my plans go sideways. It never goes as easily as I expect. I have what I think is a great plan, but something unexpected always gets in my way."

Andrea nodded. "That's because success isn't a straight, predictable path."

Alex frowned.

"Most people picture success like climbing a staircase—one predictable step after another, always moving smoothly upward. But real growth doesn't work that way. It's more like a roller coaster, full of steep climbs, sharp drops, and unexpected twists. When you set a challenging goal, you're pushing yourself beyond what's comfortable. That means setbacks aren't just possible—they're inevitable. The key isn't avoiding the tough moments; it's learning how to keep going, even when the path gets unpredictable."

She leaned forward. "The key is to *expect them*. A setback doesn't mean you have the wrong goal or that you're doing something wrong. In fact, if there were no obstacles, the goal wouldn't be challenging, would it? Challenges along the way don't signal failure. They signal that you're on the right path."

Alex considered this. Maybe all those times he had abandoned a goal at the first major setback weren't failures at all—just part of the process.

Andrea continued. "That brings us to the next part of brave action: anticipating adversity. Since brave action always comes with challenges on the path to goal achievement, it's helpful to try to predict them. Every time we set a brave goal, we also try to anticipate the adversity we'll face—both internally and externally."

Alex felt a little lost. "What do you mean by internal and external adversity? I'm not following."

"Great question," Andrea said. "Imagine someone set a brave goal of increasing lean muscle mass and getting stronger. One of the steps for achieving that goal might be working out at the gym a few mornings each week. External challenges would be a big snowstorm or a flat tire making it hard to get there. But more often than not, the real problem isn't external; it's internal. It's us getting in our own way. In this example, maybe hitting the snooze button, telling ourselves we'll go later, or choosing the comfort of bed over hard effort in the gym."

Alex considered this. "Okay, I get that. But this sounds a bit like trying to predict the future."

Andrea shook her head. "That's not possible. If it were, we wouldn't need to be brave. Anticipation is about trying to foresee the roadblocks we can, but it's also about planning our response to those roadblocks."

Alex thought for a moment. "Isn't that like focusing on the negative? I thought developing my brave mindset was about becoming more optimistic?"

Andrea smiled. "Great question. A brave mindset doesn't mean rose-colored glasses. If your goal is challenging and meaningful, you will always—and I mean always—face difficulties. That's why it's challenging and worth pursuing!"

Alex made an entry in his notebook:

Success is not linear. Anticipate the ups and downs and be ready for them.

Then he cocked his head, still unsure. "How do I plan for challenges if I don't know what they are?"

"Think of flying," Andrea said. "You can't predict if there will be turbulence or not. And you can't control it. You can't foresee a delay or a stressful flight. But you can decide in advance how you'll handle it."

Alex thought back to his flight, when Andrea was the calm stranger in 2A.

"You did those things?"

"I did. And more," she said. "When my work began to be recognized, the Institute was suddenly everywhere. And so I needed to be everywhere too. I realized that if I was going to spread the message of being brave, I'd need to fly—a lot. Which brings me to the last part of brave action: discipline."

She leaned in. "Brave action requires ruthless planning, prioritization, and focus. Daily effort. Hard goals are the easiest ones to procrastinate on, because they challenge us. It feels much easier to slip back into the comfort trap and do the easy tasks first. Brave action demands the opposite."

Alex thought of the team at Keeling. How they had slid so easily back into the habit of avoiding the difficult things.

And not just the team, he thought. *I've been just as guilty of letting the easy things run my life.*

"When you take brave action," Andrea continued, "you develop the discipline to act—to prioritize what needs to be done and to do it even when you don't feel like it. Especially when you don't feel like it. If the most important thing is the hardest thing, then you do it anyway, and you do it first."

She tapped her notebook. "Willpower and motivation erode throughout the day. First thing in the morning is when you have the best cognitive function and the highest motivation. So, you do the hardest task—perhaps the one you're dreading—*first.* Brave action means you get after it each day."

Alex thought of what awaited him back at the office. He wasn't exactly sure what lay ahead, but he knew there were going to be difficult moments.

Andrea's voice was firm. "This isn't about easing into the day. You decide your plan of attack and run at the hardest, most important task first. Imagine how great you'd feel if you'd accomplished your most challenging task for the day by 10 a.m."

She smirked. "I call this 'attacking the day'—maybe Jake has rubbed off on me. But if I'm talking to my oldest teenage daughter, I have to adjust. She'd likely roll her eyes at that phrase, so with her, we talk about 'slaying the day.' Sometimes, you've got to speak their language."

She laughed, then added, "Honestly, I love our little phrase. When I don't feel like 'attacking' my day—when I am tired and unmotivated—I think of her and decide to 'slay' the day instead. Somehow, that small shift makes it easier and motivates me."

Alex chuckled. "Trevor would probably roll his eyes at both. He calls anything he doesn't like 'lame.'"

Andrea grinned. "Sounds about right."

Alex shook his head, still smiling. He wrote in his notebook:

Attack the day—no easing in.

But as he wrote, his laughter faded as he thought about it more. "So I just have to show up and . . . grind? Get 'er done?"

Andrea nodded. "Good question. Let me answer that by first asking you something. Are you a man of your word? Do you do what you say you're going to do?"

"Of course," Alex said without hesitation.

She tilted her head. "Do you keep your word to yourself?"

Alex hesitated. "What do you mean?"

"Let's say you tell yourself you're going to do something in the morning—get up early, hit the gym, start a tough project first thing. Do you ever put it off?"

Alex exhaled, shaking his head. "More times than I'd like to admit."

Andrea leaned forward. "That's the problem. One of the most important things you can do to change your life is keep your word—to yourself. Not just for others, but for *you*."

She let that sink in before continuing. "But let's be clear—brave action is different than simply showing up to grind. It's not about pushing through mindlessly. It's about self-respect. It's about following through on your commitments to yourself. This is the purest form of self-love."

She smirked. "And yes, I just used the word *love*. Don't worry, I'm not getting soft—I just get frustrated when people get this wrong."

She shook her head. "Some people think a 'me day' means hitting pause on their goals—sleeping in, lounging around, and avoiding effort. But that's not self-love. That's self-sabotage. Because at the end of the day, avoiding the hard stuff doesn't make you feel better. It makes you feel worse."

She leaned forward slightly. "Now, don't get me wrong; rest is important. Taking a day to relax and recharge is necessary occasionally—once a week, even. It's like working out. Sometimes, a rest day is the best thing you can do to grow stronger. But too many people confuse recharging with retreating. They take too many 'me days' and wonder why they never make progress."

She sat back. "True self-care isn't about escaping effort. It's about proving to yourself that you're capable. When you push through resistance, when you check off those hard tasks, you build something more powerful than comfort—you build confidence. And pride. And nothing feels better than that—even a day of lounging on the sofa.

"If you develop your brave mindset, and you choose brave goals, then brave action should energize you. When you make progress on challenging tasks, you don't just get results—you get a dopamine boost."

Alex turned the idea over in his mind, jotting down:

Self-love is keeping promises to yourself.

"It makes sense in theory," he said, "but I'm still unsure how it can help me."

"Lucky for you," Andrea said, "Jake is here to help."

As if on cue, the door opened, and Jake, the former Marine, entered. He was as stoic as ever, but Alex noticed he wore a tight green T-shirt emblazoned with a United States Military Corps logo over the words *Pain is weakness leaving the body.*

"Nice shirt," Alex said.

"An old saying in the Marines," Jake replied, then crossed the room to the platform with the strange box.

Andrea smirked. "My younger daughter has heard me say that one a few too many times. These days, I get an eye roll whenever I bring it up."

She shook her head, amused. "But I think—deep down—she knows exactly what it means."

Alex waved back, then winced as a throb of pain shot through his arm and back muscles.

He turned back to Andrea. She held out a pair of shorts.

"These are for you," she said brightly.

Alex stared. "Why do I feel this is somehow going to be uncomfortable?"

"Trust your instincts," Andrea grinned. "The changing room is over there."

Here we go, he thought.

Five minutes later, Alex stood on the long platform at the end of the room near the first of the large boxes. Up close, he could see that the mysterious box was a covered hot tub. A short set of three steps led to the edge. He smelled a slight hint of chlorine, and the gurgle of water he had heard earlier was much louder.

Maybe this won't be so bad after all.

Jake removed the cover. The tub was full of crystal clear water, its surface rippling slowly.

"Hop in," Jake said.

With pleasure, he thought. *A hot soak will definitely help my sore muscles.*

He walked up the steps, grabbed the handrail, then turned and neatly dropped himself into the tub. He shrieked and an instant later found himself back on the platform, dripping wet.

"It's freezing!"

Alex thought he heard a chuckle from across the room, but Andrea seemed immersed in her work.

"It's fifty-five degrees," Jake said. "Optimal for health."

"Very funny," Alex said. He thought he saw a faint smile on Jake's chiseled face.

Jake held up a clipboard and pen. "What I'd like you to do now," he said, "is decide how long you'd like to stay in the tub."

"That's easy," Alex said. "Zero seconds."

Jake chuckled. "You're not the first person to say that," he said, "but tell me this: Why zero?"

"Because it's uncomfort—" Alex broke off. "I just walked right into the comfort trap, didn't I?"

Jake seemed pleased. "Good catch. What do you want to do about it?"

Alex thought back to what he had learned.

"To escape the comfort trap," he said, "I need to change how I think about hard things—that's the brave mindset."

"Right," Jake said. "How do you do that?"

Alex thought. "I need to see challenges as things that are actually helpful. Stepping stones."

Jake nodded toward the tub. "So?"

Alex looked at the cold water and shivered. "Okay," he said, "if this is actually going to help me, then . . . how about five seconds?"

Jake looked back at him, his expression blank.

"Ten seconds?"

Nothing.

"Help me out here, man," Alex said.

"Go back to the characteristics of brave action," Jake said. "First, you need a challenging, meaningful goal. Your brave mindset is only as effective as the brave action it's connected to."

Alex laughed. "What is meaningful about getting in a tub of freezing cold water?"

"How are those arms feeling?"

"Sore. Very."

"Cold plunges have health benefits, including athletic recovery. Does that matter?"

"If it helps me use my arms again," Alex joked, "I'll take it."

"Now," Jake continued, "what time in the tub would feel challenging, maybe even slightly scary?"

Alex thought about it. "Thirty seconds," he said. *Oh boy.*

Jake nodded and wrote the number on the clipboard.

"So I should just hop in?"

"Soon," Jake said. "Do you remember the next characteristic of brave action?"

"Preparation," Alex said. "I need to anticipate the challenges and decide what I'll do when I face them."

"Exactly," Jake said. "Picture yourself getting back into that water. What challenges will you face in those thirty seconds?"

Alex thought of his first brief plunge. "I think I panicked the first time," he said. "I was back on the platform before I even realized it."

"That's normal," Jake said. "I'll share a trick that will help. Before you get in the tub, I want you to take five deep breaths, exhaling completely between each one."

"Okay," Alex said, unsure.

"As you enter the water, I want you to continue that breathing. The water will still be cold—that's not your imagination. But I want you to focus on your breath. When you face the challenge of the cold, your job is to remind yourself that it's simply cold and remember that you have a plan for that."

Alex let out a breath he hadn't realized he had been holding. "Okay," he said.

He looked at Jake expectantly. Jake looked back. No one spoke.

"Oh," Alex said, grinning. "The third part. I need to be disciplined. I need to do the hard thing."

"Once you've identified the hard thing," Jake said, "putting it off doesn't make it easier. If you know something will help you reach your goal, don't delay. Take action without hesitation. That's how people become truly effective—when they know something matters, they ruthlessly prioritize it and take action, even if it's hard."

Alex looked down at the water.

"Get after it," Jake said. "It isn't going to get any warmer." Then he nodded curtly and stepped aside, motioning toward the freezing water, as if he were a maître-d' bringing Alex to the best table in the restaurant.

Alex took five deep breaths, exhaling forcefully between each one. Then he walked up the steps and entered the tub. The shock was immediate. The cold sent his entire body into contractions, and he felt an urge to scramble out.

"Remember your plan," Jake said.

Breathe, he thought. *It's just cold.*

Alex could barely expand his lungs, but he managed to inhale a slow, shuddering breath.

"Good," Jake said. "Again."

He exhaled and took another, less shaky breath.

"Good work," Jake said.

Alex closed his eyes and took another breath. Then another. *The breaths are getting easier.*

Two inhalations later, Alex was calmer. He was able to breathe evenly through his nose.

Then, just like that, it was over.

"That's thirty seconds," Jake said. "Congratulations."

He climbed out of the tub, and Jake handed him a towel. As he dried off, he was shocked to discover he was warm. As if reading his mind, Jake said, "Your body has its own form of bravery. It rises to the challenges of adversity automatically. You are feeling the legacy of millions of years of brave evolution."

Alex looked back at the tub. Then back at Jake. He felt the dull ache in his arms.

Pain is weakness leaving the body.

"Set the timer for a minute," he said.

Jake raised an eyebrow at him.

"I can do more. If we're going to set brave goals, then let's set brave goals."

Jake nodded. "Well, okay then," he said.

Alex stood a little taller. *Did I just impress Mr. Former Marine?*

He took a few more deep breaths as Jake had shown him, then stepped back into the water. It was cold, no question, but the experience was less shocking. Alex maintained his breathing and even closed his eyes.

When Jake called out, "That's one minute," Alex was surprised. *That was fast.* He remembered the sign from yesterday: *Don't Quit Until You're Proud.* He stayed in the water for an extra fifteen seconds.

When he stepped off the platform, he was grinning from ear to ear. Maybe it was the cold. Maybe it was something else. Either way, he felt . . . different. And maybe it was his imagination, but Alex could have sworn he detected the slightest hint of respect on Jake's face.

Jake gave him a firm nod. "That's solid work."

Alex's grin widened. *Did Jake just compliment me?*

Still catching his breath, Alex wiped the water from his face. "How long do most people last in here?"

Jake crossed his arms. "Six minutes."

Alex exhaled, his excitement dimming. *Six minutes?* He wasn't even close.

Jake seemed to catch the shift in his expression. "Took them months to get there."

Alex frowned. "So I'm way behind."

Jake's gaze sharpened. "That's where you're wrong."

Alex looked up. Jake took a step closer. "You think those guys started at six minutes? No. They started where you did. Probably worse. And do you know why they made it to six?"

Alex shrugged. Jake tapped the side of his temple. "Because they didn't waste time beating themselves up for not being perfect on day one. They focused on progress. And that's the secret to staying in the fight. Keep showing up."

Alex listened carefully.

Jake continued. "Becoming great at anything takes time. Strength, leadership, discipline—you don't wake up one day and have them all figured out. The people who win? They know how to keep going. And the only way to do that is to recognize how far you've come."

He clapped a hand on Alex's shoulder. "You went from panic to control. From flailing to breathing. From barely lasting a few seconds to over a minute and fifteen. You're on the right path."

Alex exhaled slowly. Maybe Jake was right.

Jake nodded toward the clipboard near the bench. "Write it down."

Is that an order? Alex wondered. Alex picked up the pen, thinking for a moment before writing:

Celebrate progress (not perfection) to fuel momentum.

He stared at the words, letting them sink in. Jake glanced over his shoulder, nodded once, and walked away. Alex looked down at the clipboard again. Maybe, for the first time in a long time, he was actually moving forward.

On his way to the changing room, Andrea gave Alex a high five, then turned to greet a group that had entered the room. When Alex returned, the group was gathered around the long row of plunge tanks with Jake. Alex took the opportunity to ask Andrea a nagging question.

"How do I do this alone?" he asked. "If Jake wasn't there to coach me, I'm not sure I would have gotten in that water."

"Remember that being brave is like a muscle," Andrea said. "You will get stronger over time. What you need most is practice. Start small, and focus on the habit of taking brave action—even if those actions are small ones. Over time, your discipline will grow. Each time you do something you don't want to do, your brain notices and builds itself up so that it will be better prepared to do that task next time. Gradually, it will be easier to do those hard things. You just have to keep showing up and doing the hard thing."

Alex remembered Jake just saying almost the same thing.

"It can also be helpful to think of the cost of *not* taking brave action," Andrea said. "Sometimes we act bravely when we know that holding back will cost us something or lead to regret."

Alex thought back to how he had declined the dream job offer from Keeling that required travel. *If I had considered the true cost of that decision, would I have been able to act bravely?*

"But," Andrea said, "none of this works without action. It's not enough to identify a challenging goal and prepare for the challenges you might face. That's just ready, aim, ready, aim, ready, aim.

"At some point," she continued, "you have to fire. You have to run straight at the hard thing and do it. Action creates momentum."

She looked Alex in the eye and held his gaze.

"You can plan to take a trip," she said. "You can pick the destination and plan for contingencies, but there comes a moment when you simply have to get on the plane."

Alex watched her leave. *It's like she's reading my mind.*

After Andrea bid him farewell, Alex left the room, his mind still spinning.

Alex felt incredible after the plunge—charged, alive. His skin tingled with the afterglow of the cold, a reminder of what he had just done. *Am I capable of more than I thought?* He couldn't wait to tell Maggie.

Maggie. In the world of cold plunges and brave action, he'd nearly forgotten that life was still happening, with or without him. He still had no idea what to do! What had Andrea really taught him? He was meeting with the team at the end of the day. Nico made it clear he had only until today. What would he tell them? He pushed open the door to exit the building, then stopped in his tracks. His arms felt a bit better. Brave action, it seemed, had a way of fixing things. He felt energized, more optimistic than ever.

Let's hope it works with the team.

TWELVE

THE GOAL

This time, Alex was the first one in the conference room. He arrived fifteen minutes prior to the 3:00 p.m. start time. But instead of the flatness that had plagued him for months, he felt energized.

Maybe this is what brave action feels like.

He had thought long and hard all day about how to explain the idea of brave action to the team. It wasn't like he could drag a tub of cold water into the conference room and ask people to jump in. He needed some other way to reach them. The more he thought about his cold plunge experience with Jake and Andrea, the more it struck him that it wasn't special. It was unusual, yes. But something was going on that was universal. Accessible to everyone.

Maybe I don't need a cold plunge, he thought. That was what had kept him working through the day, fueled by repeated trips to the coffeepot.

The team arrived almost as one. Mo was the first through the door, with a breezy hello, followed by Nico, who nodded with an expression Alex couldn't read. Raj, stout and stern, picked his usual seat. Even Willow was on time. She tapped her watch and grinned at Alex. No one spoke.

Nico took his seat at the head of the table. The uncomfortable silence dragged on for a moment. Then he looked at Alex. "Let's hear it."

Alex scanned the room and then began. "I know we're divided on what to do here," he said. "To be honest, I feel the same way."

Unreadable faces stared back.

"Yesterday, I asked you to consider the possibility that we might be able to find another way forward," he continued. "To your credit, you did. We all agreed that it would be at least possible for this team to create a prototype."

"You also said you'd come back with a plan," Raj said. "Where is that?"

Keep it cool, Alex thought. He took a deep breath, just like in the cold tub. "The board has given us six months," he said.

"And?" Raj persisted.

Alex looked at each person in turn. He could feel his heart racing. His gaze finally settled on Nico's gaunt and shiny face.

Alex said, "Let's do it in three."

Mo blurted out, "What did you say?"

Alex said a bit louder and confidently this time, "Let's build a prototype in three months, not six."

There was a brief, stunned silence.

Raj began to laugh. "You're joking, right? Tell me you're joking."

Alex had expected this. It was the biggest barrier to putting Andrea's brave action principles to work. Now, everything hinged on his next steps.

"I'm not joking," Alex said, holding up his hands. "But humor me. I have one question for you. It's short and simple, and I'd like you to each write down your answer. I think it will help us get unstuck."

He held his breath, watching for a response. He could see Nico eyeing him carefully. Mo shrugged good-naturedly. Willow wore a half-smile as if they were sharing a secret. But no one protested. Even Raj seemed to have replaced his reluctance with a little curiosity.

Phew.

Nico grabbed his notepad. "Okay, Alex. What's the question?"

"In the last sixty days," Alex began, then paused. *This better work*, he thought.

"In the last sixty days," he repeated, "when have you felt the most engaged and alive at work?"

The question seemed to catch them off guard. They all looked at each other, except for Raj, who immediately began tapping his keyboard. Ten seconds later, he closed the lid. "Easy," he said.

His lead seemed to spur the group. Nico scribbled something on his pad. Mo wrote a long sentence. Willow did too, then set her pen down. Alex held his breath. If he had made a mistake or misread the team, this would be the end. There was no way they would trust him enough to move forward. Taking the next step required buy-in, and there was no plunge pool, no pull-ups. He needed to teach the team brave action in a way they could feel. And he had to do it right now. He realized the team was staring at him.

"Okay," he said. "I'd like everyone to share what they wrote."

"I'll go first," Willow said. She looked down at her notepad and read a short sentence. Alex let go of just a little of the breath he was holding. Mo went next. Then—and Alex held his breath for this one, too—Raj, who opened his laptop and read his entry.

Finally, they arrived at Nico. He cleared his throat, then read from his note. "In the last two months," he said, "the most engaged and alive I've felt at work was two days ago while drafting the plan to present to the board."

Every head turned to stare at Alex. Every answer had been the same. It had worked. Alex could feel it. Every person in the room had been most energized and engaged at the same moment: two days earlier.

"I don't understand," Willow said. "Two days ago, we were effectively giving up. We were helping the board shut us down."

"It's true," Mo said. "We were saying goodbye to at least our current jobs. How could we all think that was the best moment of the past two months?"

Alex opened his mouth to speak, but Raj beat him to it.

"He didn't ask us for the best moment," he said. "He asked us for the most engaged and alive moment. That's different."

Raj turned to Alex. "Can you explain this?"

Alex was shocked. He had been hopeful that the plan would work, but he had never imagined that it would be Raj who first grasped the idea.

"I can," Alex said.

He spent the next ten minutes giving the team a brief overview of Andrea's principles to brave action. The notes he relayed to the team were what he had spent the afternoon on. Ultimately, his two hours of effort had boiled down to a few bullet points. But the simplicity felt right.

"So what you're saying," Nico said, "is that not only is it possible that we can create the prototype but that going about it in a brave way will improve our odds of success."

Alex nodded. "That's exactly what I'm saying. This goal matters. It's not just about the prototype. It's about proving to ourselves that we can take on something difficult and succeed. If we pull this off, we won't just save a division—we will make a positive impact to Keeling. In the process, we'll change the way we work, the way we think, and what we believe we're capable of. It's about making Keeling stronger but also making ourselves stronger in the process."

He paused, scanning the room. "But I don't just want to push forward because it's the logical next step. I want to know—does this matter to you? Do you believe this is worth fighting for?"

For a moment, no one spoke. Then Raj leaned forward, his voice quieter than usual. "I think it does. If we make this happen, we're not just proving something to the board—we're proving something to ourselves."

Mo nodded. "Yeah. We save the division, which means we save the jobs of everyone who may be impacted."

Willow crossed her arms, thinking. "It's not just another project. It's a chance to build something that actually means something."

A slow ripple of nods spread around the table.

Nico let the silence sit before he spoke. "I think Alex has helped us see something we've been missing," he said finally. "If we all believe this matters, I'd like to do two things. First, we adopt Alex's goal of getting the prototype ready in three months, not six. Second, we spend the next few hours building a plan using the brave action approach."

Alex could barely believe his ears.

"We already have a challenging goal," said Willow. "But I think there are probably waypoints. Like subgoals along the way. We should identify them and make sure they are also challenging and meaningful."

Nico nodded and made a note.

"And for each one," she continued, "we try to anticipate some of the hurdles. The *adversity*, as Alex called it."

Alex turned his head from person to person like he was watching a tennis match.

"And," Raj added, "really focus on taking action, first thing, every day." He turned to look across the table. "That really resonated with me, Alex. I feel like I can do so much more than I have been. I used to come to the office and check email for hours, get coffee, all while putting off working on the prototype. I was procrastinating. I had it backward. What you're saying feels exciting. Hard, but also exciting."

Alex was afraid to breathe.

"Well," Nico said. "Mo? Anything to add?"

Mo looked up, beaming. "I'm just so happy."

The room broke into laughter. *This is really happening*, Alex thought.

The next few hours went better than Alex could have ever hoped. The brave action approach was simple but gave them an engaging framework. Better still, Alex could feel the energy in the team. This was what he had always dreamed the development team would feel like: people rallying around common challenges, using their creativity, and engaging in positive progress. Whenever they started to become derailed, or Alex could see they were slipping back into the comfort trap, they'd pause and work the brave action principles.

By 6:00 p.m., they had a plan. It wasn't finished—there were details to work out—but it was a plan that energized Alex and the rest of the team. It was possible. He could see it right there. The rungs on the ladder, each one a step to the next. The anticipated obstacles. And scheduled meetings for checking in.

At 6:15 p.m. when he left the building, Alex felt an optimism he hadn't in a long time. *We might just pull this off,* he thought.

THE LESSON

Bravery is feeling fear and acting anyway.

- Brave action turns potential into reality.

- Brave goals challenge you—if it is easy, it's not brave.

- Success is not linear. Anticipate the ups and downs and be ready for them.

- Attack the day—no easing in.

- Self-love is keeping promises to yourself.

- Celebrate progress (not perfection) to fuel momentum.

THE

THIRD

DOOR

THIRTEEN

UNRAVEL

The team's brave action plan almost immediately exceeded Alex's expectations. It was like someone had flipped a switch marked *engagement*. Alex even heard snatches of conversation that included some of Andrea's expressions, like *everything you want is on the other side of something hard.*

He also noticed something Andrea hadn't mentioned. It seemed to Alex that the individual components of being brave—brave mindset and brave action—were somehow connected. Alex had watched as Willow took a significant step with one of the key milestones for the prototype. It was clearly a brave action on her part. Then, in the next breath, he watched her reframe an unexpected problem as an "interesting challenge." It was textbook brave action and brave mindset, and he called the Institute to speak with Andrea.

"One moment," the receptionist said, "She's in Lab 3."

The third door, Alex thought. In the excitement of the team's turnaround, he had forgotten about it.

"Alex!" Andrea said as she picked up. Alex could hear voices in the background.

"I wanted to ask you about something," Alex said, raising his voice.

"Perfect timing. My next group is just getting warmed up."

"We've been putting brave mindset and action to work," Alex said. "It feels like there's a connection there."

"You're absolutely right," Andrea said. "There are actually two things going on. The first is that there is a sequence to being brave. It's hard to take brave action without *first* adopting a brave mindset."

When Alex thought of the last two weeks, it made sense. If he hadn't understood the comfort trap and changed how he thought about challenge, he never would have been brave enough to take such a strong position with the team.

"What you are noticing," Andrea continued, "is the second thing—that the elements impact each other. A brave mindset helps you take brave action. And, the more brave action you take, the braver your mindset becomes."

That's what I saw with Willow, he thought. The more the team embraced challenge, the more they had the confidence to do hard things.

"It's a powerful feedback loop," Andrea said. "An upward spiral. Mindset to action, and back to mindset, and so on. This creates what I call the bravery effect," she added. "When we consistently choose brave actions over staying comfortable, even small ones like speaking up or taking on challenges, the effect compounds over time. Each brave choice builds momentum that transforms your entire trajectory—impacting your results, your career, and your life-satisfaction. You're already experiencing the cumulative power of repeatedly choosing courage over comfort. Just wait until you learn about the third key to building bravery . . ." She said something Alex couldn't make out. "I should go," she said, then wished him well and hung up.

———

Soon after, things began to unravel.

A critical waypoint in the team's three-month plan was to source the materials for the prototype. Alex was certain that a working product, however rough, would give the board the confidence to stay invested in their division. It was turning out to be a challenge. Recently, the team had hit their first major snag. A vendor for a critical component had pulled out. After all their productive and brave progress, it dealt a serious blow to team morale. They didn't anticipate this roadblock. Now, they were gathered in the boardroom, and tension was high.

"How do we get things back on track?" Nico wanted to know.

"I could research some new vendors," Willow offered.

"It's fine," Raj said dismissively. "I have two potential new suppliers already lined up. I just have to get them the requirements so they can quote."

"Is that something I could help with?" Alex asked.

"I've got it," Raj said. He seemed offended that Alex had asked. There was no budging him.

Alex could see that with each passing day, the team became less productive and more conflicted. Raj was digging in his heels more and more. Alex didn't think Raj was being deliberately obstructive—he just wanted to get things done on his own. Alex knew this was an essential part of taking brave action, but they were running out of time. Raj's approach wasn't the best way forward, but Alex wasn't sure what to do about it. Meanwhile, Mo was drifting like a falling leaf, buffeted by the winds of the day. It was his nature to not rock the boat. Alex suspected there was some part of the comfort trap at play, but he didn't fully understand that, either.

The rest of the team was faring no better. Willow, usually so upbeat, retreated further into her laptop with each passing day. Alex would have liked to hear more of what she thought, but she seemed reluctant to point out any problems she might be seeing. Nico, of course, was just trying to steer the ship. Alex didn't envy the role, but he could also tell that Nico was struggling. *It's like we're all rowing in different directions*, he thought. It was overwhelming. If they didn't deliver the prototype on time, he'd be packing his personal items in a cardboard box and walking out the front door.

Door.

The word appeared in his mind, blinking like a neon sign.

The third door, he thought. *That has to be what's missing.*

Alex looked around the room. Raj was in a quiet but obviously contentious conversation with Nico. Mo and Willow were focused on their screens. No amount of brave thinking or brave action was going to save them if people weren't aligned and working together.

The third door.

He reached for his phone and began to type a message to Andrea.

———

One somewhat challenging hour later, the team took a break, and Alex saw he'd missed a message from Maggie.

Our insurance renewal came in.
It's almost doubled. :[

Alex sighed. This was the type of thing that would normally be a minor inconvenience. But now, with his job on the line, the alarm bells were sounding. What if Keeling shut down the division? How much financial runway did they really have?

Runway. Alex sighed. He had been sharing all of his experiences at the Brave Sciences Institute with Maggie. It had been a wonderful way to connect, and he could see that it was inspiring Maggie. The trade-off was that Maggie had begun to talk about travel again, including the dream trip to Paris. Alex had heard her listening to French podcasts and watched her scrolling travel sites. It was wonderful to see her so inspired, but the idea made Alex's palms sweat. Could they really afford it?

And could you really handle the flight?

Alex tried to ignore the thought. But he couldn't ignore that as progress at Keeling stalled, things also began to fray at home. The early glow of possibility was being replaced by increasing stress. They had argued recently, more than once. It wasn't like they didn't disagree at times, like any couple, but these arguments were different. They had both become moody, buffeted by the stress of any given day. Their conversations were more volatile. Last night, it had come to a head.

Alex had come home, exhausted from a day in which nothing good seemed to happen. The hitch in the supplier for the prototype had put the entire plan in jeopardy. He was frustrated and, for the first time, feeling real fear at the thought of losing his job.

When he stopped for gas on the way home, he noticed the rising prices per gallon. It made him think of their tight finances. They were paying the bills—but just barely. As the tank filled, he scrolled mindlessly through his social feeds. There was a post from his old fraternity brother Dylan, who was jetting to another bigwig meeting in another European country. Everyone seemed so energized and excited about their work. Everyone except him. By the time he walked in the door, his mood had deteriorated further. That was when he found Maggie in full vacation mode.

"I found discount flights to France," she said cheerfully as he came in the door.

"Not happening," Alex had said curtly. It was out of his mouth before he even realized it.

Things spiraled from there. The conversation escalated into an argument, then a full-blown fight. Maggie was convinced that this was their one chance to get on a plane to Paris. Alex was convinced he needed to focus on work. And he was secretly terrified of the overseas flight. The combination of fears had flipped a switch in Alex. It was like two alarms flashing in his mind. *Flying! Work! Flying! Work!*

"We are not going to Paris." It came out louder than he intended.

"Maybe you're not," she said, "but I am."

She stood up. "You've been telling me all about becoming brave. What's the point if we can't do the one thing that matters to me?"

That was the end of the conversation.

Maggie had gone to bed in the guest room, and Alex had stayed up late, his mind reeling. *Everything is unraveling,* he thought. *How did we get here?*

FOURTEEN

THE SEEKER

O n his way to the Brave Sciences Institute, Alex tapped a nervous rhythm on the steering wheel. He was raw from lack of sleep, ragged from his argument with Maggie.

They had been civil that morning, and she wished him good luck with his meeting. That was something, at least. But Alex knew that his dismissal of the Paris trip had hurt her. It was her dream, and he had told her it was never going to happen. And maybe she was right. What was the point of all this bravery stuff if he couldn't just get on a plane?

He felt awful. But at the same time, he was frustrated. Why couldn't Maggie see that he couldn't do it? He couldn't be trapped in a plane like that. Overnight. In the dark. Over the ocean for hours. The thought made his stomach lurch like he was back in seat 2B with Andrea.

But Andrea did it. She learned to fly.

Still, he knew little about her. He was placing the fate of his professional and personal life in the hands of a virtual stranger. Alex thumbed back to his email and read the message from Andrea. The message asked him to review brief bios on three people in preparation for today's lesson, where he would meet the subjects of the bios—Gavin, Elena, and Marcus.

The bios were, in a word, intimidating. Each one of them seemed to have done nothing but accomplish, accomplish, accomplish. Every time Alex read Andrea's email, the words *I don't belong* kept repeating over and over in his mind.

I'm just a guy. I have a regular job. I can't even get on a plane without having a panic attack. I don't have anything to offer these people. His uncertainty had been so great that he'd even tried to cancel the meeting with Andrea. Her reply was as powerful as it was brief:

Being brave can feel scary, Alex.

She was, he knew, absolutely right. And so he had driven to the Brave Sciences Institute that morning, dreading what awaited him. Alex looked up from the draft of a message to Maggie. There were several cars parked outside the Institute. He couldn't avoid it any longer. He reread the text. It was going to have to wait. He closed the app, leaving the message unsent. It was time to walk through the third door.

The lobby was quieter today. Alex climbed the stairs to the second level, then crossed the atrium to the third set of richly polished double doors marked *Lab 3*.

The last door, he thought.

As with the first two doors, this pair contained yet another beautifully carved quote:

Associate with those who will make a better man of you.
Welcome those whom you yourself can improve.
The process is mutual; for men learn while they teach.

—Seneca[7]

Alex paused. *Easy for you to say, Seneca.* Behind these doors waited three incredibly accomplished strangers. He took a deep breath and turned the handle.

Alex wasn't sure what he had expected. In the first room, he had found a gym. In the second, a cold plunge. *A massage this time?* he joked to himself. That would be nice. But Alex knew one thing about Andrea: She specialized in discomfort. This would be no different.

What then? he wondered. *Trust falls?*

He stepped inside. This time, Alex found himself in a large area surrounded by glass-walled rooms. In each, small groups of people sat around boardroom tables, deep in discussion. The energy of the Institute struck him again—focused, intense, alive. An assistant led Alex to one of the rooms. It looked just like the boardroom at Keeling—except for the people sitting around it.

I know these people.

At first, he couldn't place them. Then it hit him. They were the strangers he had seen in the lobby of the Brave Sciences Institute on his first visit. At the far end, the young man from before—the one glued to his phone—sat, scrolling. Beside him sat the older, elegant

---

7   Seneca, *Letters from a Stoic*, trans. R. M. Gummere (Harvard University Press, 1969).

woman who carried herself like a CEO. Across from her sat the broad-shouldered man with the movie-star looks.

Alex's chest tightened. He nervously glanced around the table. Everyone looked as intimidating as their profiles suggested. *Why am I here with these people?*

"Alex," Andrea said. "Let me introduce you."

The young man looked up briefly from his phone.

"Gavin," Andrea continued. "Tech entrepreneur."

Andrea turned toward the older woman. "Elena. An accomplished leader in her field." Alex observed her for a moment, guessing she was well into her sixties, though she looked healthy enough to outrun Alex.

Andrea gestured toward the towering figure beside Alex. "Marcus. Former professional athlete." Unlike the others, Marcus looked at him and locked eyes, offering a firm nod.

Alex lowered himself into the empty chair beside Marcus and his heart sped up. He could hear it pounding. Every other encounter at the Institute had been just with Andrea and her staff. Those had been daunting—especially working with Jake, the ex-Marine. The pull-ups and the cold plunge had challenged him. But this was different. The stakes felt higher with strangers in the room. Strangers who, by every measure, were more accomplished than he was.

Is this a sick joke? The thought came unbidden. Unwanted. *Why put me in a room with people who are better than me?*

He tried to push the thought away, but the words from their bios lingered. *Athlete. Entrepreneur. Philanthropist.* Alex felt he should be delivering their coffee, not sitting at their table. Andrea, seated at the head of the table, spoke. "Let's get started."

She glanced around the room. "None of you have met, but you all share one thing in common: a desire to escape the comfort trap and become brave."

Alex snuck another glance around the room. *These people need to become brave?*

"Today, it's my job to show you that there is a comfort trap in relationships, too," she continued.

Andrea stood. "For most of human history, we couldn't survive without other people," she said. "Humans don't have sharp claws, armor, or thick hides like other species. Animals with those protective mechanisms can often survive on their own, but we can't. Our only real survival mechanism is our ability to form connections and work together with other humans."

Alex scanned the room. They were all locked in.

"To this day, one of the hardest things for us to bear is anything that might threaten the stability of our tribe." She looked around the table.

"Public speaking. Difficult conversations. Sharing an idea or a concern. At the core, our fear of these actions comes from the same place: a fear of rejection or a fear of looking weak."

Alex and Marcus exchanged glances.

"But allowing our fears to prevent us developing brave relationships," she said, looking directly at Alex, "means falling into the *comfort trap in our relationships.* It is choosing temporary ease over meaningful growth. Comfortable relationships can feel warm and fuzzy, but avoiding people who challenge us can hold us back from achieving our full potential."

She paused to let her words sink in. Alex made a note:

Prioritizing comfort in relationships prevents growth.

The room was silent. Finally, Gavin—still holding his phone—broke the silence. "To be honest, I feel like my day is filled with challenging conversations. Am I really avoiding them?"

Andrea smiled. "I'll prove it to you."

She picked up her phone. "I'm going to read four texts aloud."

Andrea started reading. By the third message, everyone knew what they were listening to. The final text was the one Alex had sent that morning to Andrea:

> Things are really chaotic right now.
> Could we reschedule?

Alex felt his cheeks flush. But every text was the same. They had all made excuses or attempted polite avoidance. These were their subtle attempts to back out, citing competing priorities. At some point, they had all tried to avoid the discomfort of today's meeting.

"When I sent you the bios," Andrea said, "I took some liberties. I presented you all in the most positive light, highlighting your greatest accomplishments."

She let the words settle. "And every one of you . . . considered backing out."

Silence. Andrea leaned in. "Your default reaction was to avoid what you felt was an intimidating or uncomfortable situation. But to your credit—thanks to your brave mindset and brave action progress—you came anyway."

She scanned the table. "You chose, in the end, to surround yourself with people who challenged you."

Alex exhaled, tension slowly unraveling from his shoulders. *Maybe I do belong here after all.*

The room was silent. Elena spoke first. "So this comfort trap—it happens when we don't have relationships with people who will challenge us?"

"Exactly," Andrea said. "That trap shows up in who we surround ourselves with *and* in how we interact with those people. We might avoid new situations, fear difficult discussions, or only spend time with like-minded people."

"What's wrong with that?" Gavin asked.

"Our friends and loved ones are well-intentioned," Andrea said, "but they often encourage comfort over challenge when what we really need is to take brave action. The people we spend the most time with may not always be the ones who push us to be brave. When I decided to start the Brave Sciences Institute, some of my closest friends thought I was crazy. They told me it was too risky and encouraged me to stay in the comfort zone—not because they didn't care, but precisely because they did. They wanted to keep me safe. But safe wasn't what I needed. I had to find people who understood what it took to build a consulting firm, people who would challenge me to keep going and who believed I could do it."

"If that's a trap," Marcus said, "how do we escape it?"

Andrea smiled and picked up a marker.

"We need to commit to," she wrote on the board as she spoke, "brave relationships."

She let the words sink in. "When we seek brave relationships," Andrea explained, "we look to connect with people who encourage us to challenge ourselves. Even if it makes us uncomfortable."

Alex wrote:

Seek relationships with those who challenge you.

"How do we do that?" Elena asked.

Andrea smiled. She picked up her marker. "Do you remember how we used the word *yet* to trigger the brave mindset? You can do the same thing with brave relationships."

Marcus asked, "What's the word?"

Andrea wrote it on the board: *seek.*

"Anytime you are stuck," she said, "ask yourself, *What brave relationship do I need to seek?*"

"I'm not sure what that means," Gavin said.

"It means seeking people who push you, encourage you, and make you better," Andrea explained.

Elena leaned in and asked, "How do we know who those people are?"

"Who scares you a bit by their success?" Andrea smiled knowingly. "Ask yourself this: Who inspires you and maybe even intimidates you a bit because of what they've achieved? Who are the people who have accomplished what you are working toward?

Andrea paused, picking up on the uncertainty in the room. "Have you ever heard the old saying, 'You become like the people you spend the most time with'?"

Heads nodded around the table.

"That is exactly what I mean," Andrea continued. "Bravery requires us to lean on others who understand our vision and our fears. To achieve your biggest goals, you have to intentionally build your brave tribe—the people who'll lift you higher, especially when your courage starts to waver. It requires bravery to approach people who may intimidate you, and even more bravery to admit you need help and support. The road to achieving hard things can get bumpy, and you will need others when you get in a tough spot. Seeking what you need is not a sign of weakness. It is a sign of strength."

"How do we do that?" Alex asked.

"We can seek brave relationships, and we can ask for feedback, help, or encouragement—whatever we need to help us keep moving forward toward our goals," Andrea explained.

"Asking for this help can make us uncomfortable," she continued. "And we often avoid it exactly when we need it most."

"I can see how it can be hard to seek feedback," Marcus said. "I learned as an athlete to seek it out, but it was difficult at first. But why would anyone avoid help or encouragement?"

"Receiving input from others can make us feel vulnerable," Andrea explained. "It activates that primitive fear of rejection."

She leaned forward. "But there's an art to it. When you ask for 'criticism' or general 'feedback,' people often hold back or soften what they really think. They worry about hurting your feelings."

"So what's the alternative?" Elena asked.

"Ask for 'suggestions to take your performance to a higher level,'" Andrea said. "This signals you're genuinely open to growth, not just fishing for reassurance. It gives people permission to be honest in a way that helps you improve."

"It also frames the conversation around future benefits rather than past problems," she added. "That subtle shift makes offering suggestions feel constructive rather than critical—for both the giver and receiver."

Alex wrote two thoughts down, struck by how the simple framing of a request could change everything:

> *Ask for suggestions to take your*
> *performance to a higher level.*

And,

> *Helping others grow strengthens*
> *both the giver and receiver.*

"There's one more thing about brave relationships that often gets overlooked," Andrea said, addressing the entire group. "We focus so much on seeking feedback and support that we forget the other side of the equation."

"What do you mean?" Alex asked.

"Offering honest feedback to someone—especially someone you care about or respect—requires just as much courage as asking for it," she explained. "When you see someone with potential making a mistake or missing an opportunity, speaking up can feel terrifying."

"That's the truth," Marcus nodded emphatically. "As a team captain, I always struggled with calling out teammates I respected. I'd think, 'Who am I to correct them?'"

"Exactly," Elena added. "What if they get defensive? What if they reject your input? What if it damages the relationship? Those fears are so real."

"I build entire systems to avoid giving direct feedback," Gavin admitted. "Anonymous surveys, team evaluations—anything to avoid the discomfort of a face-to-face conversation."

Andrea smiled at their candor. "But true brave relationships go both ways. Sometimes you're the one seeking guidance, and sometimes you're the one who needs to provide it. Both require stepping into discomfort for the sake of growth—yours and theirs."

Alex wrote in his notebook:

Offering honest feedback requires as much courage as receiving it.

As he wrote this down, Alex thought back to Raj. He clearly needed help, but he didn't want to ask for it. Alex had been afraid to give him the feedback that maybe his process wasn't working. Both of them had been stuck in the comfort trap, afraid to seek brave connection. And how about the others? Alex was sure that Willow and Mo had insights that could help the team, but they were stuck in avoiding uncomfortable conversations.

"It sounds simple," Alex said, "but what am I really seeking support for? It was easy to add the word *yet* to a sentence, but this feels more nuanced."

"You're right," Andrea said. "I like to remember a few simple questions to help prompt me. I start with *what*, then *who*, then *how*."

She wrote on the board:

> *What specific help, feedback, or*
> *encouragement do I need?*
>
> *Who has the wisdom and knowledge*
> *that might help?*
>
> *How will I ask them for the help I need?*

"But," Andrea said, "the critical thing to remember is that you need to be brave enough to seek support but also brave enough to seek it from those who can truly help you grow. Who will give it to you straight? Who will tell you what you need to hear?"

"This creating a brave tribe sounds difficult," Gavin stammered, "and intimidating."

"It's the most important part," she said. "You can surround yourself with people who will tell you everything is perfect," she paused and looked Alex in the eye, "or you can find people who help you grow and make a bigger impact."

The room fell silent. Four pairs of eyes scanned the room. Four pairs of eyes met.

Marcus was the first to speak. "If I can be brave right now, I find this all a little unsettling. And to be honest? A little embarrassing." He exhaled. "I was intimidated by all of you. I thought my problems would feel trivial or make me look weak. It is exactly as Andrea described."

Elena nodded. "Same here. But if everyone else is willing, I'd love to *seek*," she put emphasis on the word, "some feedback, help, and encouragement."

"Me too," Gavin said. "Especially encouragement. I feel like I could really use it."

Alex looked around the table, stunned. They had all felt the same way he had. For the remainder of the morning, the group spent their time seeking support. One by one, they laid out the biggest challenge they were facing—then asked for help, feedback, or encouragement.

And the responses? They were beyond helpful. Alex couldn't believe how much insight a stranger could offer. But what was most shocking were the problems themselves. Gavin, who seemed youthful and brash and so accomplished for his age, was suffering from a kind of impostor syndrome. Elena, who had more experience than anyone, was struggling to feel relevant. And Marcus, so powerful and strong, was feeling like the best of his life was behind him as his athletic years faded.

They had all been struggling. But none of them had wanted anyone to know. They had been putting on a brave face while retreating into what they knew best. And in every case, it was affecting good decision-making, their confidence, and their happiness at work and at home.

As the session came to a close, Andrea asked them each to come up with two people they would seek out for support after leaving the Institute. Alex hesitated. Then, slowly, he wrote down two names.

This is going to be hard. He exhaled and underlined the words he had written earlier: Seek relationships with those who challenge you.

"Before you all go," Andrea said, leaning back in her chair with a thoughtful expression, "I want to share something I wish I had learned sooner."

Alex raised an eyebrow, waiting.

"We've talked a lot about seeking out a brave tribe and leveraging support to achieve our biggest goals," Andrea continued. "But there's another side to it. Sometimes, in the pursuit of those goals, we neglect the relationships that matter most. Let me be crystal clear: The quality of your closest relationships is one of the biggest predictors of happiness. No goal is worth sacrificing the people who truly matter."

She hesitated for a moment, then let out a small sigh. "I learned that lesson the hard way."

Alex sensed this was something personal.

"When my daughters were very young, I was traveling constantly for work. I was passionate about what I did, and I told myself I was building something meaningful. But one day, I picked up my youngest from kindergarten, and she handed me a drawing of our family." Andrea paused for a long moment. "I wasn't in it."

There was a pang in Alex's chest.

"It was hard," Andrea admitted. "It stopped me in my tracks. I wanted to tell myself she just forgot, or that it didn't mean anything. But I knew better. I wasn't there enough for her to think of me as part of her everyday life. That moment? That was my wake-up call."

She shook her head, as if still feeling the weight of it. "I wasn't proud of it. But that's the thing about brave choices. When we realize something needs to change, we don't just sit with the regret—we do something about it. I started making different decisions. I pulled back on time away from the family. I carved out real, dedicated time at home. It wasn't easy, but it was necessary."

Andrea met Alex's gaze. "We don't just need relationships to help us grow professionally. We need them to keep us grounded. To remind us of who we are and why we're doing all of this in the first place. Our brave tribe plays an essential role in pushing us forward, but they should never get in the way of those who keep us anchored."

Alex nodded slowly. He thought about Maggie. About Trevor and Zoey. About all the nights he had come home too drained to be present. The times he had promised himself he'd make it up to them—later. Maybe later needed to start now.

As they exchanged business cards and said their goodbyes, Alex was the last out of the room. Andrea walked beside him. "I was so intimidated by the profiles," he admitted. "But once we all started being open and honest with each other, everyone just became . . ." He broke off, looking for the right word.

Andrea looked at him. "Like you?"

Alex blinked. "Exactly."

They reached the end of the hall, and Andrea turned to face him. "We are all human, Alex. We struggle. We doubt. And without exception, we find it difficult to do hard things."

She held his gaze. "When you ask for support, you're not admitting weakness. You're choosing to be brave. And in that choice, you discover something powerful: We are all fighting the same battle. Being vulnerable isn't a sign of failure. It's one of the most courageous acts there is."

She paused briefly, her voice softening. "You know, I see this all the time in my work. Some people appear incredibly confident and brave on the surface, yet vulnerability is their greatest challenge. When I work with military or law enforcement personnel, this often emerges as their biggest obstacle. But the moment they find the courage to be vulnerable—to truly open up—it becomes a profound turning point in their lives."

Alex still had his notebook in his hand. He made another note:

Being vulnerable is courageous.

He closed his pen and looked around the empty lobby. "It still feels like there's a missing piece," he said. "We set a brave goal—and I think we did a good job of it. But something isn't working. We are running out of time, and so much is riding on this." Just saying the words aloud sent his stomach into knots.

Andrea asked, "Do you remember the second lesson?"

Alex hesitated a moment, then nodded. "Without brave action, you get stuck in the dreamer stage."

"Exactly." Andrea's voice was steady. "Setting a bold goal is just the beginning. If success were as easy as writing down a goal, everyone would be winning at life. You need to follow that with action."

Alex sighed. "I know that in principle. But why is it so damn hard?"

Andrea gave a small smile. "Because it's hard, Alex. Things that matter are often hard to do. That's the truth most people don't want to accept. There's no way around it. And when the road gets bumpy, that's when you most need to leverage a brave connection."

Alex exhaled. "Everything you want is on the other side of something hard?"

Andrea nodded. "That's right. Every day, you have to ask yourself: Where do I need to be brave today? And then you need to run toward that. To charge forward. Being brave doesn't mean you don't feel fear. It means you feel it—and act anyway."

Alex swallowed. "Somehow, that feels harder to do with people."

Andrea gave him a knowing look. "Cultivating brave relationships means seeking those who will challenge you, push you, and help you grow. They won't let you off easy—they are the ones who will give you what you need to achieve your brave goal.

"That often means stepping outside of your usual circle. The people close to you mean well, but their advice may keep you safe and comfortable, not brave. You need to ask yourself: Who excels at what you're aiming to achieve? Who has walked the path you're trying to walk? Those are the people you should be seeking out."

Alex hesitated. "But that's the problem. Those people are intimidating. I'm afraid they're too busy, or that I'll be bothering them."

Andrea studied him for a moment. "You're assuming they don't want to help. But look what happened today. Think how good it felt to give support. Helping others doesn't just lift them, it lifts us, too. Connection is a two-way street. The right people won't see your call as annoying. They'll see it as an opportunity to share what they know and help someone grow. And that feels pretty great. If you didn't call, you'd rob them of that feeling and slow down your progress at the same time."

They reached the front door. Alex turned to Andrea. "One more thing I've been wondering," he said. "What did you write about me? What did my profile say?"

It was occurring to Alex that perhaps Andrea saw him very differently than he saw himself. Andrea smirked. "Ah. I'll send it to you." Then she turned and walked back toward the lab.

Alex stepped outside. The weight of everything waiting for him back at Keeling settled on his chest like a heavy stone. He needed coffee.

You can always caffeinate and think things through. The thought seemed to come from nowhere. But this wasn't random—it was what his first "real" boss and mentor, Carter, used to say.

Seek out the people who challenge you. That's what Andrea had said. *People who scare you a little.*

Why hadn't he seen it sooner? Carter was an experienced leader. Could he just call him and ask for help? Was it that simple?

Another thought hit. *Dylan.*

Dylan was an investment banker. He knew everything about credit. Keeling was obviously in financial trouble—could Dylan somehow help? Two hours earlier, Alex would have dismissed the idea outright. Corporate finance wasn't his thing. This was light-years out of his comfort zone. Dylan was an expert in that world. He had recently spent the reunion weekend with Dylan. He had his number. He had lived with Dylan, for Pete's sake. Of course he could call him.

So why was he resisting? And what about Carter? He had worked with the man for years. Carter had always said he could reach out if he ever needed anything. So why was he so afraid to simply pick up the phone?

Be honest, the voice in his head said. *Why are you really avoiding these people? Is it because they make you uncomfortable? You're assuming they are too busy and don't want to help. But helping people feels good. Maybe they'd welcome the call. Maybe this wasn't about them at all.*

Maybe this was about his own fear, staring him in the face. Alex took a deep breath, started the car, and pictured Carter's reassuring face from years ago. Suddenly, calling him didn't seem impossible— just uncomfortable. He then pressed the button on the steering wheel and said, "Call Carter Lonnings." The line rang. Alex pulled out of the parking lot. It was time to be brave.

FIFTEEN

WHAT ARE YOU AFRAID OF?

Thirty minutes later, Alex parked the car and sat staring at the Keeling building.

Carter had taken his call right away. He seemed genuinely thrilled to hear from Alex, peppering him with questions about his work, Maggie, and the kids. He was genuinely interested. Alex felt foolish for assuming that he couldn't reach out. What had he been thinking?

It was the comfort trap, of course. Andrea had been right. He wasn't avoiding Carter because he didn't want to help—he was avoiding him because asking for help felt like admitting he didn't have all the answers. It meant being vulnerable. He'd been suffering in silence when the answers he needed were a conversation away.

"You need to lead this team," Carter had said.

"But I'm not the leader. Nico is."

WHAT ARE YOU AFRAID OF?

"Leadership isn't a title, Alex. It is an action," Carter explained. "It's hard to do hard things. But that doesn't change the fact that they need doing. If you see something that needs to be said to help the team, say it. If something needs to be done, do it. The team will be stronger for it. Strong leaders do the right thing, even when it feels uncomfortable. Your team needs you to be brave—you know this is the right thing to do."

Be brave. There it was again. *It's hard to do hard things.*

Alex had been waiting for permission. But leaders don't wait. They step forward—especially in moments that matter most. His call to Dylan had gone unanswered, but just making the call felt like a win. He was done waiting. Now, he was sitting in his car outside of Keeling, staring at his phone. There was the unsent text to Maggie:

> I'm sorry. I just can't do it. I know it's important, but I just can't do the flight.

His thumb hovered over the *send* button. He heard Andrea's voice in his head: *You need to run straight at it.*

He hit *delete*, then stepped out of the car.

———

The boardroom was silent. The kind of silence that wasn't calm—it was tense. Everyone was staring at their screens, but Alex could see through the facade now. If he hadn't known better, Alex would have sworn they were all deeply engaged in saving Keeling. But he *did* know better.

What he was really seeing was a team of people all struggling alone. They were stuck in the same comfort trap he had been—mistaking "bravery" for "I don't need help."

Alex sat down at the opposite end of the board table from Nico. And then, he waited. For five long minutes, Alex just sat. He listened to the hum of the air conditioner. The soft clicking of keys. A throat clearing. A chair creaking.

One by one, the others started glancing at him. First Willow. Then Raj. Even Nico finally flicked his eyes up from his laptop.

The longer Alex simply sat there, the more awkward the energy in the room became. People started shifting in their seats. The room felt tighter, like the walls were closing in. Finally, Nico broke. "Is there something you wanted to say, Alex?"

Alex paused. At the end of their call, Carter had shared what he called his "secret weapon."

"Every time my team has been stuck," Carter had said, "the answer has always come from answering three specific questions. Every time. Without fail." Alex had pulled the car over so he could write them down. They were:

What is the obstacle holding you back right now?

Who are three people who can help?

Why aren't you connecting with them?

Sitting in the boardroom now, Alex saw how these questions fit with what Andrea had taught him. They forced you to look at discomfort straight in the eye. They exposed the exact thing you were avoiding.

He could almost hear Andrea now: *If they were easy, they wouldn't be brave.* The mysterious woman from seat 2A had an annoying habit of being right.

Alex realized that the room had grown still. Four faces were staring at him, waiting.

He took a breath. His heart began to speed up.

This is it. Take the step.

"I've been feeling stuck," he said at last. "And more than a little worried that I was leading us down a dead-end road."

He let that sit for a moment. No one interrupted.

"But then I realized . . . there are people out there who already have the answers we need."

No one spoke.

A hint of curiosity appeared in Nico's expression. Willow tilted her head slightly.

"At first, I was intimidated to reach out to them," Alex admitted. "But when I did, they challenged me to tackle the problem head-on. And it worked."

He paused and looked around the table.

"We need to start seeking brave relationships. All of us. Together."

Four pairs of wide eyes blinked back at him.

The silence dragged on for another long moment. Then, one by one, in slow, halting steps, they began to speak.

Alex looked around the room.

They were all struggling alone, even though they were sitting in the same space.

"What if," he said slowly, "we created dedicated time for brave connections? Ten minutes at the start of each meeting where one person shares their biggest challenge and the rest of us offer genuine feedback or support?"

Willow perked up. "That's actually brilliant. Instead of everyone spinning their wheels separately."

"I'm not sure about this," Raj said, though his tone lacked its usual defensive edge.

That's why it would be brave," Alex said. "It would mean being willing to say 'I don't know' or 'I'm stuck' instead of pretending to have all the answers. It's pointless for any of us to pretend we have everything under control. That doesn't help our team—it only holds us back. We're all working toward the same goal, and admitting we need help isn't weakness—it's courage."

"Precisely," Nico said, surprising everyone. "And it would save us hours of inefficient work when someone is struggling but too proud to ask for help." He glanced meaningfully at Raj, but with kindness in his eyes.

"So it's not just about getting help," Mo said thoughtfully. "It's about offering it too. Being brave enough to speak up when you see something others don't." He paused, his usual smile fading into something more reflective. "I always try to be nice—which often means staying quiet when I notice problems. I don't want to make anyone uncomfortable." He shook his head slowly. "But I'm realizing that's not actually kind. If there's something I need to know to do better, I'd want someone to care enough to tell me. True kindness might be having the courage to share the difficult truth."

Alex nodded and wrote in his notebook:

Offering honest feedback requires
as much courage as receiving it.

This was exactly what Andrea had taught him—brave relationships worked both ways. Sometimes you were seeking feedback, and sometimes you were offering it. Both required courage.

He looked around at their faces, seeing a new openness that hadn't been there before. *Maybe we're ready for this.*

"Let's put this into practice right now," Alex suggested, looking around the table. "Who wants to go first? What's your biggest challenge with our prototype?"

There was a moment of hesitation.

Then Raj cleared his throat. "The supplier issue is worse than I've been letting on," he admitted, his voice tense but determined. "I've been trying to solve it myself, but I'm hitting walls I didn't anticipate."

The room went quiet. It was the most vulnerable any of them had seen Raj.

"What exactly are you stuck on?" Willow asked gently.

As Raj began explaining the specific technical challenges, Alex watched something shift in the room. The energy changed from isolation to connection. They weren't just colleagues sharing space anymore—they were becoming a brave tribe, facing challenges together instead of alone.

After they worked through a solution for Raj, something unexpected happened.

"I've been struggling too," Mo volunteered, surprising everyone. His usual cheerful demeanor gave way to genuine concern as he outlined his difficulties with the testing protocols.

And then it was Willow, eager to get input on the interface design she'd been quietly wrestling with for weeks.

Even Nico shared a challenge about managing the board's expectations, something he'd never discussed with the team before.

By the time they wrapped up an hour later, they had not only addressed four significant problems that had been silently holding them back, but created a new way of working together. Something had fundamentally changed.

As Alex prepared to leave the office after their breakthrough session, Willow caught up with him in the hallway.

"What you did today," she said, "getting everyone to open up—it was different. Better."

Alex smiled. "Thanks. But this is just one part of brave relationships."

"What do you mean?"

"What we've done is create connections within our team," Alex explained. "But there's another critical part—developing a brave tribe beyond our immediate circle. People with expertise we don't have, who can challenge us in ways we can't challenge each other."

Willow considered this. "Like specialists in our individual functional areas?"

"Exactly," Alex nodded. "Think about it—Raj needs technical experts who understand supply chain better than any of us do. You might need UX designers who can challenge your thinking. I'm planning to reach out to Dylan, my college roommate who works in finance. He might have insights about funding options we haven't considered."

"That's . . . actually brilliant," Willow said. "Building connections both inside and outside."

"The key is seeking people who you look up to and trust," Alex said, recalling Andrea's words. "People who've accomplished things you aspire to. Then being brave enough to ask for their help."

Willow nodded slowly, her eyes growing distant as if already mentally cataloging her own potential brave tribe. With a quick smile, she turned and walked back toward her desk, clearly lost in thought.

———

Alex sat in the car, staring up at the windows of the house.

Inside, he knew Maggie was waiting.

She would almost certainly still be angry. And she would be right to feel that way.

What am I supposed to do?

He replayed the scenes back in his head. The group session at the lab. The moment in the boardroom.

It had gone better than he could have hoped. Clunky at first, but real. There had been moments of defensiveness and difficult conversations. But by the end, they had gotten somewhere. They had moved forward.

Alex could feel it. And see it! Within an hour of their brave connection, things just seemed to flow. They had compiled and clarified the requirements for the critical component.

Even Raj—who had admitted that he needed help with the job but was afraid to ask—was more engaged than Alex had ever seen him. And then, after the meeting, something shocking had happened.

Raj had thanked him.

"Happy to help," Alex had said. And he meant it.

But now he was home. Standing in his driveway, he felt something unexpected: He'd rather be back at work trying to save the entire division than walk inside and face his wife.

You're brave enough to tackle that—but not this?

He almost laughed. But wasn't this exactly what Andrea had warned him about? *There is a comfort trap in relationships, too.*

He took a deep breath and stared at the front door. Was he really about to be the guy who ran toward hard things at work but avoided them at home?

No. Not anymore.

He got out of the car and walked to the front door.

Maggie was in the kitchen. Her shoulders were stiff.

She wasn't looking at him.

He hesitated. But then, he crossed the kitchen and stood in front of her.

"Hey," he said.

"Hey," she replied.

Seek.

The word flashed in his mind.

You have to do the hard thing with people, too.

Maggie hadn't been in the meeting with Andrea. She didn't know anything about brave relationships—at least not in the way Andrea had explained it. But that didn't matter.

He took a slow, steady breath and reached for her hand.

"I'm sorry," he said. "I didn't mean what I said yesterday."

Maggie didn't respond. But she didn't pull her hand away.

"I am really struggling," he admitted. "But instead of telling you that, I've been shutting you out. I didn't want to seem weak. I should have checked my ego at the door."

Maggie didn't speak, but he saw her nod her head. *Yes,* the nod said, *you should have.*

He took a breath. "Can you help me find my way back to us?" he asked quietly. "I'd like to hear more about Paris. I think . . . I think that might be something good for both of us."

Her eyes welled with tears.

Then she nodded.

And went to him.

FROM ALEX'S NOTEBOOK:

Ask for support from those who will challenge you to be your best.

- Prioritizing comfort in relationships prevents growth.

- Seek relationships with those who challenge you.

- Ask for suggestions to take your performance to a higher level.

- Helping others grow strengthens both the giver and receiver.

- Offering honest feedback requires as much courage as receiving it.

- Being vulnerable is courageous.

THE
LEAP

SIXTEEN

CRISIS

One evening, while Maggie and Zoey were at the park, Alex knocked on Trevor's bedroom door.

"Hey, kiddo," he said. "How's it going with recess?"

Trevor shrugged. "I remembered what you said—about how I could get better if I kept trying. And I did try. Really. I went out for recess every day this week."

"That's great," Alex said. "I bet that was hard at first."

Trevor nodded. "It was, a little. It's easy to stay inside at recess. But . . ." He trailed off.

"But?"

"Well, I'm still not very good," Trevor admitted, "so no one asks me to be on their team. And if I don't get picked, I don't get a chance to get better."

Alex frowned. "That's tough." He walked in and sat down on the bed before continuing. "You know, I actually had the same problem at work."

Trevor's eyes widened. "You have recess at work?"

Alex laughed. "Okay, not exactly the same problem. But I was feeling stuck—just like you."

"What did you do?"

"I asked the smartest person I knew for help," Alex said.

Trevor blinked. "That sounds easy."

Alex smiled. "It wasn't. I was really nervous."

Trevor tilted his head. "I wouldn't be nervous asking someone really smart for help."

Alex raised an eyebrow. "Really? What if it was someone really good at sports? Maybe one of the really good players at school you know? How would it feel to ask them for help in soccer?"

Trevor hesitated. "That would be pretty scary," he admitted.

Alex nodded. "Yep. And let me tell you a little secret: I learned today that when you ask people for help, it makes them feel great. Especially when they're really good at something."

Trevor eyed him skeptically. "Really?"

Alex grinned. "Hey, have I ever steered you wrong?"

Trevor smirked. "What about that time you told me to try the hot sauce?"

Alex held up his hands in defense. "Okay. Fair enough." He laughed, then ruffled Trevor's hair. "Even dads are allowed to make one mistake."

Trevor smirked. "Sure, Dad. Just one."

———

Becoming brave was certainly working at home, but Alex was most surprised by how brave relationships were paying off at work. The entire team was thriving. The idea of seeking support in ways that were challenging seemed to be a lubricant—everything ran faster and more smoothly. Slowly but undeniably, they were becoming more vulnerable.

Nowhere was the change more apparent than in Raj. The idea of brave connection seemed to transform him. The previous day, Alex had arrived to find Raj and Willow laughing like kids. "Oh good," Raj said with a grin. "You're just in time, Alex."

It's been a while since Raj smiled at me, Alex thought.

"I was just telling Willow I was struggling to ask for help, but I never realized why. I thought it was because no one else could do the job properly. I thought I was a perfectionist."

"Wellllll," Willow said jokingly. They all laughed.

"Okay. Maybe that too." Raj chuckled. "But now I understand why being brave was so hard for me. I just didn't want to seem weak. I ended up approaching a senior manager in another division."

Willow smiled at him, clearly delighted. "What happened?"

"She was so helpful! I was intimidated—just like Alex said. The most unexpected thing was that she seemed sincerely interested in the prototype and was excited to offer advice. She wants me to follow up and let her know how it goes. She mentioned that we need more cross-division collaboration."

It's exactly as Andrea predicted, Alex thought.

The entire team was thriving. Last week, finding a new supplier for a critical prototype component had been their biggest challenge. It had seemed insurmountable. They solved it in a single day simply by being brave. The willingness to ask for help and feedback was so powerful that Alex found it hard to believe they had functioned without it.

The more they leaned into this approach, the more natural it became. As trust grew, so did their confidence. Asking for help and offering feedback wasn't just accepted; it was expected.

We hadn't, he thought. *And neither had I.* It was true. Occasionally, Alex would catch himself saying or doing something he would never have done before meeting Andrea. He was, he realized, becoming brave.

He was part of something special.

For the first time in a long time, he felt energized and excited to work at Keeling.

And then, just like that, it all fell apart.

———

Alex knew something was wrong the moment Nico entered the room.

His face was pale. He was sweating. From across the table, Alex caught Willow's eye. She saw it too. Nico moved to the head of the board table and stood silent. One by one, the team members stopped what they were doing.

"What is it?" Willow asked.

Nico took a breath. "The board convened an emergency meeting this morning," he said. "They have made a decision."

A pit opened in Alex's stomach. "A decision about what?" he asked.

Nico hesitated, then, finally, answered. "They've decided to terminate the project."

Every mouth fell open. For a moment, no one spoke. Then everyone began talking at once. The room exploded.

"How could—"

"But we're so—"

"That's not fair—"

Nico held his hand up in a "don't shoot the messenger" gesture. The room grew quiet. "They've tried to find additional funding for the project but couldn't find a partner," he explained. "The financial situation is worse than they realized. They're speeding everything up."

Willow's voice was small. "What does that mean for us?"

Nico sighed. "They'll find spots for us in other divisions. Over the coming weeks, you'll all be reassigned."

The silence was deafening.

Alex looked around the room as the team processed the news. Raj was staring blankly at his screen. Willow's hands were clasped so tight her knuckles were white. For probably the first time ever, Mo was frowning,

Terminate the project?

Just a few weeks ago, a part of Alex might have welcomed the news. Now, it felt like a punch in the gut. For all of the ups and downs in the past few weeks, Alex had felt alive. All from learning about and applying the three keys to being brave.

And now, it was over. He watched the team members gather around Nico. No one noticed as Alex slowly pushed back his chair and stood. No one saw him grab his phone and step out into the hallway.

He just needed air. And to think.

———

Alex had expected the usual short drive to the Brave Sciences Institute. Instead, the address Andrea had sent was well outside the city. The round-trip drive would take him more than two hours, if traffic cooperated.

In the meantime, he couldn't imagine what the team was thinking back at Keeling. He'd left them talking about their possible reassignments, pestering Nico for details.

Meanwhile, Alex was going to do . . . *what, exactly?*

He had reached out to Andrea in desperation. *Maybe there's a fourth door*, he thought, *or a secret basement level, like in a spy movie.*

But the farther he drove, the more ridiculous the idea seemed.

Who was he kidding? The project was over. They'd tried their best. It hadn't worked out, but Alex had learned more in the past month than he had in years. Wasn't that enough?

He was likely going to be reassigned, not laid off. Wasn't that a win?

His hands tightened around the steering wheel. He should turn back. Go back to the office and get to work.

But get to work on what?

His knuckles were white. His mind bounced back and forth as he drove.

Turn around. Keep going. Turn around. Keep going.

His foot hovered over the brake.

He kept going.

There was no question that for the past year, he had been shrinking. Not just at work but in his personal life, too.

Andrea had changed that. She had opened something in him.

Like a Pandora's box. Except this box was full of good things. Powerful things.

Ideas about being brave that worked. Principles that changed things. Bravery had an effect on him—in so many ways.

He reviewed Andrea's research in his mind, counting off the points on his fingers as he drove.

- First, there was avoiding hard things makes you weaker, ensnaring you in a comfort trap: Almost everything you want is on the other side of something hard.

- Then, there was brave mindset: Bravery begins with how you think.

- Next was brave action: Brave action turns potential into reality.

- Finally, there were brave relationships: Seek out those who challenge you and call forth your best. You need your brave tribe on your journey to achieve your goals.

It all made sense. The bravery effect Andrea had described was real—he could feel how each brave choice had built upon the previous one, creating momentum that was transforming not just individual situations but his entire trajectory. There was no question it helped. But in the end, it wasn't enough.

And who is *this woman, anyway?* Alex tried to ignore the thought, but he couldn't. It had been lingering there all along. Andrea was an enigma, a kind of black box. She had simply helped—never pushing, never expecting anything in return. *Why?*

His phone chimed.

Your destination is ahead on the right.

Alex rounded a bend in the country road. A gravel turnoff appeared. He slowed the car and pulled in. Then he saw the sign:

HARCOURT AIRFIELD

Everything inside him seized. "No," he said aloud. "Hell no."

Through the windshield, he saw an open chain-link fence, leading to a runway.

"Absolutely not," Alex reaffirmed.

Beyond the fence, Alex could see the low, squat shape of an aircraft hangar. A long runway vanished into the distance. Beside the hangar, a tall pole held a wind sock that drooped in the still air.

His heart pounded. *She wouldn't.*

But, of course, she had. Andrea knew what his greatest fear was. And now, she was going to force him to face it. He felt like an idiot. How had he not seen this coming? Alex started breathing faster. He slammed the car into reverse.

Nope. No way in hell. Enough was enough. He'd return to Keeling, and they would all face reality together. He gritted his teeth, putting the car back into drive. His foot rested on the brake.

Just leave. Go back to work. There is nothing left to prove.

Then, as if in a movie, Alex saw his future play out before him. If he turned back now, he knew exactly how the next few weeks would unfold. He'd go back to Keeling to face reality. The project would shut down. They'd all be assigned to new positions. He and Maggie would build their savings. They would start college funds for Trevor and Zoey. They would work. They would be fine. Live their lives.

The future would be safe. Predictable. Fine.

But we won't ever go to Paris. You'll never be able to take a job that requires travel. His stomach twisted. His foot stayed on the brake.

No . . . The thought sliced through him.

Maggie won't learn French.

And Trevor? Zoey? What won't they do?

In their safe, predictable, and comfortable life, what would they all never do? His fingers trembled on the steering wheel. And for the first time in his life, he hated the answer.

SEVENTEEN

NO WAY

*I*t's not a big deal. Planes are safe. Safer than cars.

Alex repeated the phrase like a mantra as he walked toward the small terminal building.

It's not like you never fly, he told himself. *You just hate it. You're terrified, but you can still do it.*

But as he looked through the glass building, his confidence wavered. Parked on the other side, in front of the terminal, Alex could see a half dozen small airplanes. It hit him: There would be no giant jumbo jet with its comfortable seats and soothing entertainment system. There'd be no in-flight service. No champagne. These were small aircraft, with tiny doors. Noisy. Bumpy. And they only had one engine.

Just one.

His mind jerked into red-alert mode, the planes seeming to shrink before his eyes, becoming so tiny that they couldn't possibly hold themselves aloft, never mind carry a few grown adults.

His heart pounded as he reached the door of the building. Alex tried to calm himself. *Everything you want is on the other side of something hard.* He thought of Trevor. Zoey. Maggie. He took a few deep breaths. Then he pulled open the door and walked inside.

The first thing he saw was Andrea, smiling broadly. And for a moment, the tightness in his chest eased just a little. *It's going to be okay,* he thought. *You've got this. You can be brave.*

Then he saw Jake stride into the terminal, as stoic as ever. And he saw that Jake was wearing some sort of jumpsuit. Alex's shrinking, anxious mind did weird gymnastics. *It's a costume party,* he thought. *And he's Elvis. In a jumpsuit.*

But it wasn't that, of course. It was so much worse.

"Is this a joke?"

Inside Alex, some switch had flipped. One moment he was afraid, the next he was angry. Livid.

"Alex—" Andrea began.

Alex cut her off, pointing at Jake. What Alex had thought was some kind of costume was a skydiving jumpsuit. Over it, strapped tightly, was—well, Alex knew exactly what it was. It was a parachute.

"This is some kind of joke for you, right?" Alex's voice rose. "A sick joke? You take people, you find their fears, and then you push, and you poke, and you—" he broke off, looking for the right word. "You *prey* on them. Is that it?"

Jake stared at Alex, startled by the accusation.

"Alex—" Andrea tried again.

"Then comes the pitch, right? The money part." Alex let out a sharp laugh. "I should've seen it. This whole thing—teaching us to be vulnerable, telling us it will make us brave—it's just a *setup.*" He practically spit the word out. "A way to break us down so you can build us back up in your program. I'm just a prospect, and this is how you close the deal."

Silence. Andrea didn't blink.

"What happened at work?" she asked.

"Why do you care?"

Andrea looked at him. "Why do you care?" she asked. Her voice was soft but insistent. "You came here," she persisted. "Why?"

Some of his anger began to fade. *Why had he come?*

The answer popped into his mind: *Seek.* The lesson of the third door.

"I came for help," he said. Then added, "From people who challenge me."

"Then let us help," Andrea said.

Jake left the two of them alone, and Alex relaxed further. He set his backpack down and grabbed his trusty notebook before Andrea led him out the front of the building, and they walked the pavement. Sunlight glinted off the shining surfaces of the parked planes as Alex told her the news of the shutdown.

Alex watched as a couple walked from a hangar toward a small aircraft.

He stopped and turned to Andrea.

"Something has been bothering me," Alex said. "Were you really afraid of flying? Or was that just some story?"

He held his breath. He didn't think he could bear for it all to be a lie.

Andrea made a small *hmmm* noise. Alex saw her shake her head ever so slightly.

"I wasn't always," she said. "But one night I was on a red-eye flight after a long work trip. This was when the Brave Sciences Institute was in its early days. It may be hard to believe, but we were once a small, struggling consultancy."

She looked out at the runway.

"I was exhausted," she said. "The meeting hadn't gone well, and we were at the edge financially. We really needed the contract. Then my flight was delayed for hours. On top of the work stress, I missed my daughter's dance recital, which I'd been trying to get home for. By the time I got on the plane, I was a nervous wreck.

"The flight was awful. The worst turbulence I've ever seen. At one point, all the power in the cabin went out and the plane dropped thousands of feet almost instantly."

She looked at Alex.

"I thought I was going to die."

Alex's stomach churned at the thought. *Maybe I shouldn't have asked.*

"That was how it started?" he asked.

She nodded.

"I had to cancel four meetings in the next six weeks. And those were meetings we could not afford to cancel. We were right down to the wire with our creditors, and I couldn't even open the flight app on my phone, never mind actually fly."

"What did you do?"

She laughed. "I used my tools. I focused on what I knew about being brave. I began to slowly shift my mindset, reframing flying as an opportunity to grow again. I set a brave goal—to fly again in a month. And I reached out to make a brave connection."

She smiled at the thought. "I actually called my competitor, of all people. Another researcher who understood the science as well as I did. It was incredibly humbling. But also incredibly helpful."

"And then what?"

"Then the day arrived for the flight," she said. She paused, her eyes distant. Alex held his breath.

"And then I couldn't do it," she said.

I knew it, Alex thought. *She's just like me. Afraid.*

Then Andrea shrugged. "So I did it anyway," she said.

Alex stared at her, dumbfounded.

"Sometimes, you just have to do the hard thing."

Alex felt something inside him loosen. "Flying was obviously critical to your work," he said. "But do we have to face every fear? Maybe I don't need to fly. Or skydive, for that matter."

"Yes, I was motivated. Plus, it's hard to take a researcher seriously when they don't follow their own evidence," she said with a chuckle.

Alex nodded. It was a fair point.

"Not every fear is worth facing," she said. "But some fears? Some fears own you. They lead you instead of you leading you. Those are the ones that define you. I just knew I had to face that fear."

"You knew that if you didn't fly, you'd never get your life back," Alex said.

She looked off, past the runway, past the airplanes, and into some faraway distance. "I knew that if I didn't fly," she said, "I would never live. This was a powerful motivator. As much as I was terrified of flying, the thought of losing my business and not doing the work I was so passionate about was worse. The pain of regret I would face was much greater than the discomfort of flying. Sometimes thinking about the consequence of not doing the brave act is the most powerful motivator."

As they talked, they slowly circled the concrete apron where the planes were parked, eventually returning to the terminal door. Alex stared at it. *Another door,* he thought. He thought more about what Andrea had just said, writing in his notebook:

The pain of regret is the greatest risk of all.

"To answer your question," Andrea said, continuing their conversation after a moment's pause, "No—you don't have to face every fear to lead a fulfilling life. Not at all. Becoming brave is about choice."

"How so?"

"Our choices eventually define us," she said. "Our lives become the accumulation of those choices.

"Sometimes, you're faced with a choice to be brave, and you decide not to. That's fine. No one is asking you to live on the edge every second of every day.

"But some choices matter. They have an outsized influence on our lives. Think of them as *Brave* with a capital *B*. They are the choices that send your life in a different direction. The decision to start the business. To take the new job. To have the scary conversation."

Andrea paused. "I bet you can think of some of those," she said.

"I was just thinking of my son, Trevor," Alex said. "When Maggie and I discussed having kids, we kept getting caught up in details. Could we afford it? Was now the right time? What about our careers? Looking back, those things seem so trivial. Eventually, we just decided it was too important to us. We had to do it."

"That's a beautiful example," Andrea said. "How would you feel right now if you hadn't made that decision?"

Alex answered immediately. "Like I'd missed out on an essential part of my life because I was afraid."

Andrea nodded. "When we turn away from those big, brave moments," she said, "something happens. The decision to not face your fear changes you. You become the person who didn't take the new job. Didn't have the difficult conversation.

"Sometimes," she said, reaching for the door handle, "you become the person who lives with the pain of regret." She opened the door and stood holding it.

"And that," she finished, "turns you into someone very different."

Alex stared at the door.

"This isn't my choice to make," Andrea said. "No one can be brave for you. And let me be clear: I have no judgment around this. This is your life."

Through the glass, Alex could see Jake standing in the terminal lobby. Alex thought he could see a look of concern on his normally stoic face. At last, Alex turned back to Andrea and said, "I never thought of myself as someone brave enough to jump out of planes."

Andrea nodded. "We are all the heroes of our own lives," she said. "Sometimes we just need to be reminded. Sometimes, the obstacle of achieving what you want is you."

The hero of my life, Alex thought. It had a nice ring. He thought of Keeling and all of his friends and their jobs. He thought of Maggie and Trevor and Zoey. He turned to Andrea. "What do you do," he asked, "when you know the right decision, but it still seems so hard?"

"You leap," she said.

And then she walked inside. Alex didn't follow her immediately. He stood in silence for a moment, before jotting down another line in his trusty notebook:

To avoid regret, you must be willing to leap.

He followed Andrea into the hangar.

EIGHTEEN

ONE SECOND

Looking back, Alex would swear he had no memory of walking through the door. One moment, he was watching Andrea walk into the terminal building, feeling a tightness in his chest as if he were being squeezed by an enormous vice; the next, he was in a two-hour orientation session, wearing a jumpsuit just like Jake's.

Jake was explaining what was about to happen. How they would ride together in a small plane. How the plane would have no door. *No door!* How they would do something called a tandem jump, which meant that Alex would be tightly strapped to Jake, who would deploy the parachute when they jumped from the plane. *Jumped from a plane!*

Alex felt as if his mind had split in two: One part listened and tried to prepare for what seemed insane, the other part floated above it all, watching curiously as it unfolded. That second part of his mind seemed strangely unperturbed that Alex, Jake, and Andrea were now walking across the concrete toward a small plane, its engine running.

A pilot sat behind the controls, wearing headphones. A woman in a similar set of headphones greeted them and motioned them to climb aboard.

Alex's detached mind watched him actually climb aboard. There were no seats, he noticed—his heart racing a little faster—and they sat on the floor of the plane, like cargo in a hold.

The copilot climbed inside and buckled in.

Alex felt a sudden urge to talk. To free his mind from the constant vigilance of watching everything. Now he understood why Andrea had wanted to speak to him on their first flight together.

In that moment of overwhelm, she had needed to say something. He had to raise his voice against the growing noise of the plane's engine.

"How do you know?" he yelled.

"Know what?" Andrea shouted back.

"If it's worth it," Alex yelled. "All the bravery. It's so hard. How do you know it's worth it?"

Andrea didn't hesitate.

"You don't!" she called back. "Leaps are like faith. You have to believe without knowing!"

She grinned and gave the waiting copilot the thumbs-up. The plane began to move ahead, taxiing to the runway. When it finally stopped with a jolt, Alex realized they were pointing down the runway. His stomach churned.

He saw the pilot push the throttle slowly forward, and the noise of the engine grew. The wheels rumbled against the pavement.

He looked back at Andrea, his voice strained.

"If you knew how things would work out," she yelled as the engine began to roar, "you wouldn't need to be brave."

The words hit like a punch.

The noise of the engine grew until it was too loud to speak.

The wash of the propeller blew through the open door.

Then the pilot released the brake, and the plane lunged ahead. Alex watched in sick fascination as the ground outside began to flow past the open door. Soon, it was moving so quickly that all the details of the runway—the cracks and discolorations, the grass alongside, the markings—all merged into one seamless blur.

And then—the plane lifted off.

Immediately, the bumpiness decreased, but a sensation of pressure replaced it. The force of the climb pressed Alex back against Jake. He risked a glance out the open door and felt his stomach drop.

The world was shrinking below.

The trees, the hangar, the tiny dots of cars—all falling away.

He squeezed his eyes shut.

A few moments later, the plane leveled off. The pilot eased off the throttle. Despite the open door, the noise dropped to a level where they could speak again.

Jake's voice came from behind him. "How are you doing?"

Alex swallowed. "I don't feel ready," Alex said. "I—" He broke off. *What else was there to say?*

Jake's voice was steady. "If you wait until you feel ready, you'll wait forever."

The words made sense.

But the pressure in his chest kept rising. A building need to escape.

He turned his head toward Andrea and spoke, his voice firm.

"Take me back."

Andrea shifted on the floor of the plane to face him. "If that's what you want, that's what we'll do," she said. "But will you give me two minutes?"

Alex exhaled sharply. His pulse was pounding in his ears.

"Two minutes," he said.

"Most of what we call *courage* isn't what you think," she said. "It feels like a huge thing, but it isn't. Bravery is tiny."

Alex risked a glance out the open door. *Was that a cloud?*

"It doesn't feel tiny," he muttered.

Andrea smiled. "That's the trick. The courageous part is the split second it takes to do something that changes you. It only takes a few thoughtful words to start a long conversation that can change your life.

"Bravery isn't a marathon," she continued. "No one is brave every second of every day. Courage is more like a series of connected sprints. Short bursts of faith."

Alex shook his head. "I appreciate what you're trying to do here," he said. "And—you've been amazing. But I don't think that's going to help.

"We followed the framework. We've changed our mindset, taken brave action, and come together as a brave team. I'm afraid it wasn't enough."

Andrea nodded but said nothing.

"Right now, my team needs me," Alex said. His voice was resolute now. "And I don't think I can explain to them, or my family, why I'm doing"—he waved his arm at the plane—"this when we're in the middle of a crisis."

He sighed. "I thought you'd have a fourth door. Some final

strategy. But not only is there no fourth door," he nodded at the hole in the wall of the plane, "there's no door at all."

Andrea's expression softened. "It's true," she said. "Each element of the Building Bravery framework is like walking through a door. A threshold, moving from comfort to discomfort. Every time we cross that threshold, we find courage. We discover our brave selves. We become more than we ever imagined by passing through those doors, over and over, day after day, in tiny ways. In our decisions to embrace challenge, to rise to challenging goals, and to connect courageously. Each step forward changes you. We don't just achieve more—we become more. Yes, many people seek bravery because they want better performance or career advancement. But they soon realize bravery is about so much more. It's about who you become on the journey itself.

"Here's the thing, Alex. Each of those doors leads to the same room. Each brave step we take, however small, brings us to the same place."

"What is it?"

"Freedom," Andrea said simply.

Alex stared at her.

"Being brave is the ultimate expression of freedom. It's how we free ourselves from fear. From self-limiting thoughts. From regret.

"It's how we accomplish things we are proud of. And it's how we bring out the best in ourselves and others by being brave enough to be vulnerable together.

"Being brave," Andrea said, "will set you free.

"Not just freedom from fear—but the freedom to stop letting life happen to you and start steering your own path," Andrea continued.

"Bravery gives you back the wheel. It's how we move from drifting through life to choosing it. That's what agency is. That's what this entire journey is about. Bravery transforms you from a passenger in your own life to the one who charts the course.

"But sometimes"—she nodded at the gaping door—"the price of that freedom is a single, crazy, brave act."

She exhaled. "I know you want there to be a fourth door, something predictable. But doors? Doors are easy. Doors let us keep one foot firmly on the ground while we decide."

Andrea tilted her head toward the sky.

"Sometimes," she said, "you don't get a door."

She met his eyes. "Sometimes, you simply have to leap."

A green light flicked on above the open door. Alex's stomach clenched. He was in the clouds. He could see them, wispy and white, floating past like something out of a dream. It didn't seem real. His breath was labored. His fingers dug into his jumpsuit.

"So," he said at last, "no fourth door."

Andrea shook her head. Her expression was peaceful and reassuring, like it had been on the flight the day they met. *The flight. That seems like so long ago,* Alex thought. *But also like yesterday.*

"There is," she said, smiling at him, "just a place we all arrive at if we are brave enough."

The pilot said something over the headphones, and Alex felt himself being shifted as Jake maneuvered them toward the open wall of the plane. He tried to calm his racing heart, but it was like a wild animal he couldn't control. The plane banked, turning left, and his stomach lurched as he realized he was staring down toward the ground. He saw tiny houses and, in the distance, the narrow strip of the runway.

Jake spoke into his ear. "When you're ready, lean forward and let yourself fall. I'll take care of everything else."

Alex looked down.

He wondered if he could see his house. His family safely tucked inside. Andrea's words came into his mind: *You become the person who has regret.*

The plane banked again, sending another nervous flutter through him.

"That's enough," he said aloud.

He closed his eyes. He imagined his family: Maggie, Travor, Zoey. Andrea's voice again. *Everything you want . . .*

Alex took a deep breath. He opened his eyes. ". . . is on the other side," he whispered.

And then—he jumped.

———

The car was right where Alex had left it, pointed away from the airfield as if poised for escape. For some reason, it surprised him. Everything else had changed in the last hour, so shouldn't this? The car should be gone, driven away in another lifetime, by another Alex. But it was still here. Waiting. Right where he had left it.

And so are your problems, he thought.

All of their financial troubles remained. His job, his team—they were teetering. And yet, he was calm. Maybe it was adrenaline leaving his system. Maybe it was something more. Alex's thoughts felt clearer as he climbed into the car. A few hours ago, he had sat in this very seat, heart pounding, squeezing the steering wheel so hard that his knuckles had gone white.

Now? His breath was slow and easy. His fingers rested lightly on the wheel. Then, he grabbed his pen and notebook, while the experience was still fresh. He wrote:

*Every brave leap brings you
closer to your true self.*

He studied the line. That was what Andrea had said, but it didn't completely sum up how he was feeling now, after he had taken his own big leap. He jotted down one more thought:

Bravery is the ultimate form of freedom.

His mind was at peace. Alex looked through the windshield. The sky was a perfect blue. A single cloud hung in the sky. *I was there,* he thought. A quiet certainty settled over him. In that moment, he knew exactly what to do at Keeling. But first, there was one more thing.

He picked up his phone, tapped on the screen, and opened an app.

NINETEEN

CHOICE

That morning, the team had been energized. He could feel it. It was as if they had developed a collective brave mindset, momentum building with each step. Each part of Andrea's framework—brave mindset, brave action, brave relationships—amplified the others. It wasn't just productivity. It was engagement.

Alex had never felt more *alive* at work. That was the word. Becoming brave was bringing him alive. And it wasn't just the skydiving.

Certainly, jumping from a plane had been euphoric. Just as Andrea had said, it took only a brief moment of courage for him to step from the door. The initial shock was overwhelming—a violent rush as they exited the plane, his body tumbling momentarily before Jake stabilized their position. The wind roared past with incredible force, pressing against his face and chest. But after those first few disorienting seconds, something unexpected happened. The free fall sensation transformed. Rather than feeling like he was falling, Alex felt like he was floating on a powerful cushion of air. Time seemed to stretch. The fear was still there, but alongside it emerged an indescribable feeling of freedom—of flying rather than falling.

Then, Jake deployed the chute, and the world went quiet.

In that moment, it was as if everything Andrea had said coalesced into one singular experience. Brave mindset. Brave action. Brave relationships. The challenges at work, the fear of an uncertain future, the distance at home—all of it vanished. As his heartbeat had slowed, he realized he was floating. Below him, rather than a terrifying fall, the world spread out like a tapestry.

It was quiet. Serene. Peaceful.

In that instant, he became *free*.

It was one of the greatest feelings in his life.

It wasn't about the height. It was about the overwhelming feeling of being alive, of having made a difficult choice and watching his life open up because of it.

When they landed, Alex had stood on solid ground with a new certainty. He was filled with a sense of accomplishment beyond anything he had ever experienced.

I jumped out of a plane. He had stared up into the sky, wondrous. *I did it.*

The feeling had enveloped him all the way back to Keeling. For the entire drive, he felt electric. Glowing. As if light poured from the windows of his car and spilled out into the world.

Everything felt possible.

It was just as Andrea had said it would be. Brave actions create ripples. They spread through your life, making other challenges seem smaller. One act of courage made another possible. And over time, you could change everything.

Yet, as Alex walked into the conference room now, he was seeing the opposite.

The momentum had stopped.

There was a stack of file boxes in the corner of the meeting room. Nico was erasing a whiteboard. Mo pulled charts and spreadsheet printouts from the wall. Willow was packing up a projector. It was as if the entire room were shrinking.

"Hello," Alex said.

Everyone turned. Willow studied him. "What happened to you?"

Alex looked around the room. "Can we sit down for a moment?"

Just a few weeks ago, he would have seen the board's decision to terminate the project as final. That was how life worked, after all—someone told you your next step, and you took it. You could quibble about the terms, sure, but the next step was the next step. It was a single path, winding ever onward.

But now, Alex had begun to see the truth in Andrea's words.

Becoming brave is about choice.

That was what being brave meant. Understanding that life was always giving you a choice. That everything was optional. Bravery wasn't about pull-ups or cold plunges or even skydiving; it was about recognizing that every moment held a decision: Stay safe? Or step forward.

The realization was blazing in his mind now, as bright as the sun. The essence of bravery was choice. And they had a choice now.

Alex had been staring at the board table, lost in thought. He looked up to see his entire team watching him, waiting. He looked at each one in turn, then leaned back in his chair and nodded once.

"I have an idea," he said.

The pushback was immediate. He'd expected it. He'd prepared for it.

But he'd never been more sure. He felt completely, utterly at peace with his decision.

Each of them now had a choice to make.

The freedom is in choosing and then letting go, he thought.

Bravery wasn't about being certain of the outcome. It was choosing the path anyway. Freedom came from knowing you chose the brave path, no matter where it led.

Bravery wasn't about whether you won or lost, succeeded or failed. What mattered was the courage to believe and try. To push past the edge of your comfort zone and grow.

"I don't understand," Mo said. "The board shut down the project."

Alex nodded. "Yes, they did."

Mo raised his palms. "So what are we even talking about?"

Raj stared at Alex like he'd lost his mind. "Are you trying to get us fired?"

Alex shook his head. "I'm only trying to do one thing: to see this as a choice."

"But it's not a choice," Mo said. "The board decided. They are reassigning us."

"They decided," Alex said. "But they haven't reassigned us." He paused. "Yet."

Nico's eyes narrowed in thought.

"It's going to take a couple of weeks to sort this out," Alex continued. "What are we going to do with that time?" He motioned to the boxes scattered around the room. "Take two weeks to do two hours of packing?"

Alex looked around at them and smiled. "I'd like to do something that scares me," he said. "Just a little."

This time, Nico noticeably cocked his head and studied Alex.

"You want to keep working on the prototype," Willow said.

"I want to finish it," Alex said. "And I want your help."

Silence.

That's good. It means they see it as a choice.

Nico finally spoke. "If I may, I can summarize what Alex is saying. He's asking us to be brave."

"It sounds like he's trying to get us fired," Raj said.

Nico raised his hand. "Technically, all the board has said is that they are discontinuing the project and that we are all going to be reassigned."

Willow smiled. "But they never told us what to do in the meantime."

"No," Nico confirmed. "They did not."

"So what if we keep going?" Mo finished.

They sat in silence.

Alex noticed he was holding his breath.

"It's not risk free," Raj said at last. "We're not aligning with the board's intention."

Alex nodded. He had thought of that on the drive back.

"You're not wrong, Raj. There is a possibility that we face some kind of consequence."

Raj nodded. Mo too.

"But we could also succeed," Alex said. "We're so close."

"How do we know if it will work?" Mo asked.

"We don't," Nico said.

"There's no way to know for sure," Alex agreed.

"So what do we do?" Willow asked.

Alex shrugged. "We choose," he said.

"To follow the board," Willow said.

There was a long pause.

"Or leap," Alex said.

They looked at each other.

Finally, Nico spoke. "There are some things at stake here. I don't feel I can make this decision for us. Let's take some time to think it through," he said, standing and gathering his things.

"We meet back here in thirty minutes to vote."

———

An hour later, Alex walked to his car.

The next step was one he needed to take in private. He unlocked his phone, scrolled through his contacts, and hesitated for only a moment before tapping his name. The line rang once. Twice. He was holding his breath. Just as he was about to hang up, he heard the familiar voice of his old college roommate.

"Alex!" Dylan's voice was warm, familiar. "I'm so glad you called. I've been thinking about you."

"You have?" Alex had been certain that Dylan didn't have time between private jet flights or boardroom deals.

"Since the reunion," Dylan said. "I realized how much I miss talking to you. I mean . . . we used to live together."

There was a pause. Then Dylan's tone shifted, quieting.

"Truth be told, I've been going through a rough patch. This job is . . . It's hard. Brutal. The hours, the competition. My marriage is—" He exhaled. "Shaky."

Alex blinked. "I—I had no idea."

"I've been meaning to call," Dylan admitted. "Just thought maybe I should reach out, you know? You always seem like you have everything figured out."

Alex let out a sharp laugh before he could stop himself.

"I cannot imagine anything further from the truth," Alex said. "Honestly, I was calling you because I thought you had everything all figured out. I should have called ages ago."

"Why didn't you?"

Alex hesitated. *Sometimes, you have to leap.*

He took a breath. "I was jealous of your life and didn't want to talk to you."

Alex held his breath.

Dylan was silent for a moment. Then, to Alex's surprise, he let out a deep, genuine laugh.

"Brother, you can have my life anytime you want," he said, and then they both were laughing—loud, unrestrained, real laughter.

When they finally stopped, Alex felt something shift inside of him. The weight of the past few months, the doubt, the distance—it had lifted. Alex felt a warm glow spread through his whole body. *This is what bravery really feels like,* he thought.

"Listen," Alex said, "I'm calling for a reason. I need help."

———

The house was dark when Alex pulled into the driveway.

The decision was made. In a matter of days, it would be over. And yet, Alex was completely at peace. *This is what leaps are like,* he thought. *You jump, and then everything is out of your hands.*

He picked up his phone, tapped an app, and glanced at the screen. Everything was as he'd left it. Beside him on the passenger seat was a small, beautifully wrapped package for Maggie. He picked it up, stepped out of the car, and walked inside.

In the kitchen, he carefully set the package on the counter, propping it against the coffee maker so that Maggie would see it first thing in the morning. He had a feeling he wouldn't be the first one up in the morning. He smiled, imagining her saying, "Merci" when she opened it. Then, he climbed the stairs.

He paused outside Trevor's room. The door was slightly ajar, and in the dim glow of the hallway light, Alex could see him sleeping soundly, tangled in the covers. He slipped into the room and sat on the edge of the bed.

"Hey, kiddo," he whispered. Trevor slept on. Alex swallowed against the lump rising in his throat. "This might be a weird thing for a father to say to his son," he murmured, his voice thick. He exhaled slowly, feeling the unfamiliar sting in his eyes. "But I think you would have been proud of me today."

He sat for a very long time, listening to the steady rhythm of Trevor's breathing, watching the peaceful rise and fall of his small chest. As he sat there, Alex reflected on how much had changed in just a few weeks. He could see now the two possible paths his life could have taken. Had he continued choosing safety and comfort at every turn—avoiding difficult conversations, declining challenges, staying in his lane—he would have slowly contracted, becoming less confident, less capable, more trapped. Instead, the brave choices he'd made—pushing against the board's decision, jumping from a plane, reconnecting with Dylan—had created the opposite effect. Each act of courage had expanded his sense of what was possible, building momentum that carried into the next challenge. This, he realized, was the true bravery effect. Consistently choosing courage over comfort, even in small moments, gradually transformed not just his circumstances but who he was becoming.

Then, quietly, he stood, bent over, and gave Trevor a kiss on top of his head. He walked down the hall, climbed into bed, and for the first time in what felt like forever, Alex closed his eyes and immediately fell asleep. A deep, dreamless sleep.

THE LAST LESSON

You always have a choice.

- The pain of regret is the greatest risk of all.

- To avoid regret, you must be willing to leap.

- Every brave leap brings you closer to your true self.

- Bravery is the ultimate form of freedom.

THE OTHER SIDE OF HARD

A lex checked the address in his phone and looked up at the building in front of him: *37 rue de la Bûcherie, 75005 Paris.* This was the spot, no doubt. But why this spot?

Before leaving for Paris, in the whirlwind of packing, wrapping up work, and getting Trevor and Zoey off to their grandparents, Alex had meant to message Andrea. But he hadn't. Not until the long overnight flight when his thoughts had returned to a lingering question. He tapped out a message to Andrea, simple and direct:

Why did you help me that day on the plane?

He had sat beside countless strangers in his life. Many of them, he was sure, were as successful as Andrea. Not one of them, that he could recall, had ever expressed concern for his well-being the way she had. Not one had invited him into their world or helped him transform his life.

Andrea's response was quick:

When you arrive at *37 rue de la Bûcherie,* look over the door.

He was here. Alex looked again at the building.

The address marked the home of the legendary Shakespeare and Company bookstore. From outside, it was as charming as he would have imagined—colorful, crammed with books, its facade weathered with history. Small café tables lined the sidewalk, offering a view of the Notre Dame Cathedral across the river.

"Go ahead," Maggie said. *"Je vais nous trouver une table."*

She beamed at him. Alex smiled back.

She was glowing. In the few days they had been here, she had devoured the city. Her French seemed to be growing by leaps and bounds. She belonged here.

Alex turned back to the store.

Look over the door.

At first, he saw nothing of note above the entrance. Then, stepping inside, his eyes caught the inscription over an old wooden doorway within the shop. It looked to be hundreds of years old. Beside it was one of the innumerable bookshelves that filled the building. Over the doorway was a sentence:

"Be not inhospitable to strangers,
lest they be angels in disguise."

Alex smiled. *Brave relationships.*

This was the unexpected part of becoming brave: You started to see the world through a different lens. You discovered there were opportunities to be brave—in mindset, action, and relationships—everywhere. Challenges—things that once felt intimidating—transformed into opportunities. They were like strangers—angels in disguise.

He pulled out his phone, snapped a selfie with the doorway in the background, and sent it to Andrea. And then he added another photo, a shot taken from under the wing of a plane, midair. In it, Alex and Maggie were both spread-eagled, free-falling through the sky. Below them, barely visible, was the shoreline of France, and on it, the beaches of Normandy. He and Maggie had visited several days earlier—a trip that had been on her bucket list for years, as her great-grandfather had history here. It also seemed a fitting tribute to bravery.

Even now, Alex found it hard to believe it was him and Maggie in the photo. *Just weeks ago, I said this was impossible*, he thought.

That was *the power of choosing to be brave.*

And it wasn't just him.

Alex had watched, with grateful surprise, as the ideas of being brave had taken hold with Trevor. He was now not only a full participant in recess, but Alex had overheard him talking to his younger sister as she struggled to climb a tree in the park.

"I know it's hard," Trevor had said to her, "but being brave makes your life bigger."

That's exactly what Andrea had been teaching him all along—the bravery effect in action. Each time we face a choice—speak up or stay silent, step forward or step back—we're shaping our future selves. The cumulative effect of repeatedly choosing comfort had once been shrinking Alex's world, limiting his career, dampening his confidence, and distancing him from Maggie. But the opposite was equally powerful. Small brave choices compounded over time, creating an upward spiral where each courageous act made the next one slightly easier. And Trevor was teaching these lessons to his little sister.

Little Zoey had nodded at her older brother as if he were a wise old man holding the secret to life. Then she proceeded to scale the branches like a monkey. Alex could only marvel at how a ten-year-old boy had captured the entire essence of becoming brave.

Being brave, Alex realized, was infectious.

He and Maggie had stayed awake long into the night on the overseas flight to Paris, talking for hours. Their conversations felt new again—exciting, full of possibility.

Tucked into the plane seat, Alex could see the book he left for Maggie the night the team had decided to make the brave choice: *French for Beginners.*

Inside it, he had placed two plane tickets to Paris.

Business class, even. The tickets weren't in the budget, of course. But during their call, Dylan had insisted they use his bottomless supply of airline points to upgrade. Alex's first instinct had been to refuse. But then he thought of Andrea and realized that Dylan was trying to help. When he'd accepted, he'd never heard Dylan so pleased.

At the airport, he'd sent Andrea a photo of their boarding passes: seats 2A and 2B, of course.

Here's to being brave, he'd written.

His fear of flying wasn't gone. It popped up at the most unexpected moments. Checking their luggage. Browsing a magazine rack. During a gate change. Each time, he would feel a sense of unease move through his body like a wave. But then it would pass. He would remind himself of everything he had learned. Most of all, he would remind himself of an unusual woman who had helped him after facing her own fear. The woman who had taught him the power of being brave.

Alex took one last look around the bookstore before stepping outside, wanting to take it all in. As he turned, a section labeled *Philosophy* caught his eye. He paused.

All those quotes Andrea used at the Brave Sciences Institute . . . They were Stoic philosophy quotes, he realized. Out of curiosity, he walked over.

On a whim, he picked up a book titled *How to Be a Stoic: Ancient Wisdom for Modern Living.* He flipped through a few pages and was immediately intrigued.

Maggie's waiting for me outside. Still, something about it pulled him in. Without overthinking, he walked to the checkout and bought the book.

Maybe I should finally learn what this Stoicism is all about, he thought, tucking it under his arm as he stepped back into the Paris sunlight. I'll understand how to talk in riddles. Alex spotted Maggie seated at a table outside. He sat beside her and gazed in wonder at the towering sight of Notre Dame. She was flipping through a French book. Alex's phone chimed. It was Nico.

It had worked. The team had unanimously voted to keep going and finish the prototype. They had worked tirelessly for another two weeks, pushing ahead despite the board's decision to shut down the division. And when they finally presented the prototype? The board members were more than impressed. The prototype was not only done but had features that would differentiate their product from that of their competitors. It had exciting potential. Alex was impressed too. He had never imagined they could accomplish so much so quickly.

Then came the missing piece. Dylan had come through with a

lifeline. His firm couldn't help, but he had connected Alex with a high-level commercial bank in their state. Based on Dylan's recommendation and the prototype's potential, they were willing to meet with the executive team to discuss becoming a financial partner.

The board, once certain of shutting down the division, now had an unexpected decision to make. Two weeks earlier, they'd had no product and no money. Now, they might have both. It might be enough to tip the scales. It was still early, but the Keeling development division looked like it was back in business.

Alex read Nico's email:

> **Alex,**
>
> Congratulations on your new role. I can't think of anyone better suited.
>
> I also wanted to express my gratitude. We would all be in a different place if it wasn't for you. Not only would I not have this role—a role I only got because of the brave principles I learned from you—but I might be out of a job altogether.
>
> **Bravely yours,**
> **Nico**

Alex exhaled, shaking his head with a smile.

We'd all be in a different place.

Once the board had understood how the team had been so successful, everything began to change. First, Nico surprised Alex by taking a brave step. He pitched the board on bringing the principles of the Brave Sciences Institute across the entire organization—with him as the driving force. The board had agreed and allocated a budget almost immediately. Nico claimed it was the fastest the board had ever agreed to anything.

And with Nico stepping into that new role, that left an opening for the head of the development team. Nico pushed Alex to take the role. Alex had declined, for two reasons.

First, he knew someone better suited: Willow. She was born for this. She was brave by nature and a gifted communicator. Alex couldn't think of a better combination for the leader of a team focused on innovation.

And second? Alex had already received a better offer of his own. *And a braver one,* he thought.

When he and Maggie returned from Paris, Alex would start a new role at Keeling. He had been offered the dream job that he'd turned down just the previous year. The irony wasn't lost on him. A year ago, he had turned down his dream job because it involved flying. Yesterday, he'd once again voluntarily jumped out of a plane. If there was a greater testament to the power of becoming brave, Alex didn't know what it was.

Now, looking around the streets of Paris, he soaked it all in. He was sure he'd made the right choice. Andrea's ideas had transformed his life. It was the most exciting opportunity Alex could imagine. And it scared him just a little. *The perfect amount,* he thought. For the first time, it seemed possible to have work that energized him. He really could wake up Monday and be excited about the week ahead—if he was brave enough.

Maggie, too, had found her footing. She'd made her own brave choice that went far beyond learning French. She had chosen to go back to school, to pursue her doctorate in education. It was a dream she'd held for years, always questioning herself: *Am I smart enough?* Now she'd made the brave choice to take her career to the next level, moving from the classroom into administration and curriculum design to make a bigger impact.

Andrea's bravery framework had changed all of it. It had changed all of them. Alex turned off his phone and tucked it away. He wouldn't need it this week.

"Everything okay?" Maggie looked at him, concerned.

Alex stared across the Siene at the beautiful cathedral. It was stunning.

He looked at Maggie. She was radiant. He'd never seen her so happy.

"Everything," he said, smiling and taking Maggie's hand, "is *magnifique.*"

THE END

ACKNOWLEDGMENTS

First and foremost, my deepest gratitude goes to my husband, Jonathan. Your unwavering support, patience, and belief in me carried me through every chapter of this journey. To our daughters, Brooke and Sydney—you inspired me to write this book, and I hope these pages always remind you to embrace bravery in all areas of your lives. You both make me incredibly proud.

I'm profoundly grateful to my mentors. You have been my brave tribe, challenging me, guiding me, and encouraging me along the way. I would not be where I am today without you.

Marty Seligman, thank you not only for your groundbreaking research but also for your encouragement and the inspiring discussions we shared about bravery. Your early belief in my manuscript affirmed its importance and fueled my motivation.

Ken Blanchard, your mentorship over the past decade has been invaluable. Thank you for always believing in me and my message, especially during times when I doubted myself. Your encouragement to write this book made it a reality.

Dr. Cynthia Pury, your insights and expertise deepened my understanding of the science of bravery and ensured the parable was scientifically sound. Your thoughtful guidance challenged me to think differently, greatly enhancing the book.

Jon Gordon, your generous time, wisdom, actionable advice, and continuous support have been instrumental in helping me bring the message of bravery to the world. Thanks for showing me the path and believing in the message this book brings to the world.

To all the incredible thought leaders, researchers, and authors whose work has profoundly inspired my journey, thank you. This book would not have been possible without your pioneering research and valuable contributions. I have learned everything from you. I am deeply honored to have built upon your ideas and insights, and I hope this book continues to carry your important work forward.

Special thanks to my rockstar story architect and creative partner, Dan Clements—working with you was truly amazing. Your remarkable talent, thoughtful collaboration, and unwavering dedication helped bring my vision vividly to life, weaving the science of bravery seamlessly into a compelling narrative filled with relatable characters and powerful lessons. To the extraordinary team at Greenleaf Publishing—your guidance, deep expertise, and infectious enthusiasm made my first publishing experience incredibly rewarding and enjoyable. Thanks for patiently showing this rookie the ropes and making the process an absolute joy.

Heartfelt appreciation goes to Zack Kristensen, my strategic advisor for the book launch. From navigating the writing process and finding the right publisher to crafting a successful launch plan, you were my rock—always just a phone call away whenever I felt uncertain, confused, or overwhelmed. Your wisdom, steady guidance, and strategic insights have been truly invaluable.

To my wonderful beta readers—your honest feedback, thoughtful insights, and unwavering encouragement strengthened this book in immeasurable ways: Jonathan Schulman, Cynthia Pury, Jeanne Zucker, Joella Hopkins, Jason Godley, Kim Lancaster, Timothy Gerrits, Barbara Prichard, Curtis Morely, Irena Powers, Catherine Divine, Jodi Wellman, Kristen Lessig-Schenerlein, Tracy Heinemann, Elaine O'Brien, Jay Graves, Zhenya Evans, Ginger Johnson, Sherri Fisher, Blair McHaney, Kathryn Britton, Myra Roldan, Amira Leifer, Ginger Collins, Laura Leaton, Rich Drengberg, Charlotte DeLavalle, Rephael Houston, Mike Ettore, Randee Flynn, Marty Evans, and Jessica Hart.

A special thank-you to the extraordinary MAPP community at the University of Pennsylvania. Your passion for Positive Psychology continuously fuels my work. To my beloved "MAPPsters"—your bravery, friendship, and intellectual camaraderie have enriched my life deeply. Many of you have become cherished friends and mentors who share my passion for exploring the science of living our best lives. Those who've especially impacted my journey—you know who you are—please know how deeply I appreciate you, your friendship, and your support.

Thank you to my incredible clients and colleagues. Your support and trust have allowed me to bring my research to life. Your stories, challenges, and triumphs inspire me daily and drive my mission to help others unlock bravery in their lives.

To my family and friends—I love you all. Your endless love,

support, laughter, and encouragement have made this journey not only possible but joyful.

Finally, thank you to my readers—for your curiosity, your commitment to growth, and your courage to seek exciting opportunities that challenge and stretch you. My greatest hope is that this book ignites your bravery, empowers you to boldly pursue your path to greatness, and enriches every dimension of your life. This book is dedicated to you.

THE SCIENCE
BEHIND THE STORY

I didn't invent bravery.

Thinking, acting, and connecting bravely is as old as humanity itself. For as long as we've existed, we've faced challenges—not only to survive but to grow. Bravery isn't just an admirable trait; it's essential. In many ways, it's nature's engine for progress.

I'm also not the first person to study or write about bravery. The ancient Stoics—think Seneca, Epictetus, and Marcus Aurelius—were among the earliest to redefine *courage*. Instead of reckless daring, they saw bravery as grounded in wisdom, self-discipline, and resilience. Thanks to thinkers like the Stoics, we now understand that bravery isn't just for warriors and explorers; it's something anyone can cultivate in daily life.

Fast-forward to today, and we have an ever-growing body of scientific research that backs this up. Studies in psychology, neuroscience, and positive psychology all reinforce what the Stoics knew intuitively—bravery is a skill that can be developed, and it's directly tied to success, resilience, and overall well-being.

The ideas, frameworks, and conversations between Alex and Dr. Andrea Hastings in this parable are not just inspiring—they're grounded in real science. Each insight, strategy, and transformation moment has roots in robust research.

I'm passionate about sharing this because cultivating bravery has genuinely transformed my own life. I'm experiencing it even now, writing this book despite fears of criticism, rejection, or failure. It feels both terrifying and exhilarating—which, I've learned, is exactly how meaningful growth should feel. Every time I've stepped into discomfort, it's led to breakthroughs I couldn't imagine and helped shape the person I am today. I've witnessed the same in countless clients and students who've moved from hesitation to bold, confident action.

Everything in this book is backed by science. The insights here aren't just personal opinions—they're supported by robust research. Bravery, whether in mindset, action, or relationships, is foundational to living a fuller, richer life. The lessons shared aren't solely my own. I stand on the shoulders of brilliant researchers and thought leaders who've uncovered not only what bravery means, but how to develop it. Bravery isn't reserved for a few special people—it's available to everyone willing to learn and practice it.

If you love knowing the "why" behind the story—digging into the fascinating science and incredible minds behind these concepts—keep reading. I've highlighted key thinkers, landmark studies, and groundbreaking insights that shaped this book. This isn't every study I reviewed, just the curated "greatest hits" that profoundly influenced the concepts, models, and tools you've explored.

If the deep dive into research isn't your cup of tea, no worries! Skip ahead to the QR code at the end, and grab the free resources waiting for you. Either way, I'm grateful you're here—together, let's put bravery into action.

WHAT IS BRAVERY, AND WHY DOES IT MATTER?

Bravery is not about being fearless; it is the choice to act despite fear toward a meaningful goal or something that aligns with your values. It's not just about feeling courageous; it's about developing the ability to step forward even when doubt creeps in.

Christopher Peterson and Martin Seligman identified bravery as a core virtue in human flourishing, emphasizing that courage is essential for overcoming challenges and living a meaningful life. Their research on character strengths laid the foundation for understanding bravery as a skill that can be cultivated.

Peterson, Christopher, and Martin Seligman. *Character Strengths and Virtues: A Handbook and Classification.* American Psychological Association, 2004.

———

Dr. Cynthia Pury has extensively researched the psychology of courage, exploring how individuals perceive and enact courageous behaviors. Her work highlights that courage is subjective—what feels brave to one person may not to another. She also examines how personal values and situational factors influence our willingness to take bold action.

Pury, Cynthia, and Shane Lopez. *The Psychology of Courage: Modern Research on an Ancient Virtue*. American Psychological Association, 2010.

———

Neuroscience supports this as well. Bruce McEwen's research on neuroplasticity shows that facing challenges rewires the brain, increasing our resilience over time. Stress, when harnessed effectively, actually makes us stronger.

McEwen, Bruce. "Physiology and Neurobiology of Stress and Adaptation: Central Role of the Brain." *American Physiological Society Journal* 87, no. 3 (July 2007): 873–904.

———

Similarly, Lev Vygotsky's "Zone of Proximal Development" demonstrates that true learning and growth happen just beyond what we already know and can do.

Vygotsky, L. S. *Mind in Society: The Development of Higher Psychological Processes*. Harvard University Press, 1978.

———

All of this sounds great, right? A simple "Be brave! It makes you stronger!" pep talk should be enough. But it's not. People *want* to be braver—but they need to know how. According to Ryan Niemiec, bravery is one of the top character strengths that people want to develop. They recognize its value, but simply telling them to stop being a coward doesn't work.

Niemiec, Ryan M. "Mental Health and Character Strengths: The Dual Role of Boosting Well-Being and Reducing Suffering." *Mental Health and Social Inclusion* 27, no. 4 (November 30, 2023): 294–316.

BRAVE MINDSET: REWIRING THE WAY WE THINK

Bravery starts with believing that we can change and grow. Carol Dweck's research on growth mindset proves that intelligence and abilities are not fixed—they can be developed through effort, learning, and persistence.

Dweck, Carol. *Mindset: The New Psychology of Success.* Ballantine Books, 2006.

———

We often fear stress, but research shows that how we think about stress determines its impact. Alia Crum and Kelly McGonigal's work demonstrates that when we view stress as a tool that helps us rise to the challenge, we actually become stronger.

Crum, Alia, Peter Salovey, and Shawn Achor. "Rethinking Stress: The Role of Mindsets in Determining the Stress Response."

Journal of Personality and Social Psychology 104, no. 4 (2013): 716–33.

McGonigal, Kelly. *The Upside of Stress: Why Stress Is Good for You, and How to Get Good at It.* Avery, 2015.

———

The Yerkes–Dodson Law explains that moderate stress enhances performance—too little leads to complacency, too much leads to overwhelm.

Yerkes, R. M., and J. D. Dodson. "The Relation of Strength of Stimulus to Rapidity of Habit-Formation." *Journal of Comparative Neurology & Psychology* 18 (1908): 459–82.

———

Bravery is easier when we believe in a better future. Martin Seligman's research on learned optimism shows that optimistic people recover faster from setbacks.

Seligman, Martin. *Learned Optimism: How to Change Your Mind and Your Life.* Vintage, 1998.

———

Positive emotions can be generated, broaden our perspective, and build resilience, as seen in Barbara Fredrickson's work.

Fredrickson, Barbara. *Positivity.* Harmony, 2009.

And Ethan Kross's research on self-talk shows that how we speak to ourselves shapes our confidence and actions.

Kross, Ethan. *Chatter: The Voice in Our Head, Why It Matters, and How to Harness It.* Crown, 2021.

BRAVE ACTION: MOVING FROM DREAMER TO DOER

Bravery isn't just about taking risks; it's about staying the course. Angela Duckworth's research on grit shows that long-term success isn't about talent or luck; it's about passion and perseverance for meaningful goals.

Duckworth, Angela. *Grit: The Power of Passion and Perseverance.* Scribner, 2016.

Bravery requires setting the right kinds of goals—ones that stretch us while remaining achievable. Research in self-determination theory shows that autonomy, mastery, and purpose drive sustained motivation.

Deci, Edward, and Richard Ryan. *Intrinsic Motivation and Self-Determination in Human Behavior.* Plenum Press, 1985.

———

Many people set goals but fail to act. Gabriele Oettingen's work on mental contrasting and WOOP (wish, outcome, obstacle, plan) provides a research-backed way to bridge the gap between intention and execution.

Oettingen, Gabriele. *Rethinking Positive Thinking: Inside the New Science of Motivation.* Current, 2014.

———

Our ability to make decisions and push through challenges declines over time. Roy Baumeister's research on decision fatigue and willpower depletion explains why morning is the best time for deep, focused work. If bravery is about doing the hard thing, then the best way to set yourself up for success is to do it first—before distractions and fatigue take over.

Baumeister, Roy, and John Tierney. *Willpower: Rediscovering the Greatest Human Strength.* Penguin Press, 2011.

———

Bravery requires focused effort. Cal Newport's research on deep work explains why eliminating distractions fuels extraordinary achievement.

Newport, Cal. *Deep Work: Rules for Focused Success in a Distracted World.* Grand Central Publishing, 2016.

BRAVE RELATIONSHIPS: BUILDING A TRIBE THAT FUELS GROWTH

Surrounding ourselves with the right people accelerates growth. Adam Grant's research on prosocial support highlights how giving and receiving feedback fuels success.

Grant, Adam. *Give and Take: A Revolutionary Approach to Success.* Viking, 2013.

Grant, Adam. *Hidden Potential: The Science of Achieving Greater Things.* Viking, 2023.

———

Shelley Taylor's research on stress and connection shows that seeking social support strengthens resilience and performance.

Taylor, Shelley, Laura Klein, Brian Lewis, Tara Gruenewald, Regan Gurung, and John Updegraff. "Biobehavioral Responses to Stress in Females: Tend-and-Befriend, Not Fight-or-Flight." *Psychological Review* 107, no. 3 (2000): 411–29.

———

Brave individuals don't just accept feedback—they seek it out. Ashford and Cummings's research shows that people who proactively request feedback perform better and grow faster than those who wait passively.

Ashford, Susan, and L. L. Cummings. "Feedback as an Individual Resource: Personal Strategies of Creating

Information." *Organizational Behavior and Human Performance* 32, no. 3 (December 1983): 370–98. https://doi.org/10.1016/0030-5073(83)90156-3.

————

A sense of belonging fuels perseverance. Jean Twenge and Roy Baumeister's research demonstrates that social exclusion can undermine resilience, while connection strengthens it.

Twenge, Jean, Kathleen Cantanese, and Roy Baumeister. "Social Exclusion Causes Self-Defeating Behavior." *Journal of Personality and Social Psychology* 83, no. 3 (2002): 606–15. https://doi.org/10.1037/0022-3514.83.3.606.

————

Bravery includes knowing when to lean on others. Heidi Grant's research shows that people underestimate how willing others are to help and that seeking support strengthens relationships.

Grant, Heidi. *Reinforcements: How to Get People to Help You.* Harvard Business Review Press, 2018.

————

Brené Brown's work on vulnerability reinforces that asking for help is not a weakness but a strength. Those who embrace vulnerability build deeper connections and achieve more.

Brown, Brené. *Daring Greatly: How the Courage to Be Vulnerable Transforms the Way We Live, Love, Parent, and Lead.* Avery, 2012.

Mentorship matters. Eby et al.'s meta-analysis confirms that having mentors improves job satisfaction, career success, and personal confidence.

Eby, Lillian, Tammy Allen, Sarah Evans, Thomas Ng, and David DuBois. "Does Mentoring Matter? A Multidisciplinary Meta-Analysis Comparing Mentored and Non-Mentored Individuals." *Journal of Vocational Behavior* 72, no. 2 (April 2008): 254–67.

ANCIENT WISDOM: THE STOIC FOUNDATIONS OF BEING BRAVE

The Stoics teach that comfort is the greatest enemy of growth. A soft life makes a soft person. Strength comes from struggle, from choosing the hard path, from doing what others won't. Hardship isn't something to avoid; it's something to seek out. The more we train ourselves to endure discomfort, the more we prepare for life's inevitable challenges.

Bravery isn't the absence of fear; it's action in spite of it. The Stoics remind us that what stands in the way becomes the way. Every obstacle is an opportunity to grow stronger, to sharpen our discipline, to prove to ourselves what we are capable of. Fear and hesitation will always be there, but they do not have to control us. The only way to build courage is to act despite doubt, to step forward even when every instinct tells us to stay where it's safe.

You don't wait to feel brave. You act, and bravery follows. A person becomes courageous by doing courageous things—again and again, until it becomes who they are. Marcus Aurelius didn't wake up every day feeling ready to lead an empire. He prepared for resistance. He trained his mind to expect difficulty. He didn't ask for an easy life—he made himself strong enough to handle a hard one.

Surround yourself with those who demand your best. The people around you shape who you become. Walk with the weak, and you will act small. Surround yourself with those who challenge you, who push you, who live with courage, and you will rise to their level. The strong don't go it alone—they sharpen each other. Seneca put it simply: "Associate with those who will make a better man of you."[8]

The Stoics didn't just talk about bravery; they lived it. They didn't believe in waiting for the perfect moment, the perfect mindset, or the perfect opportunity. They believed in showing up, every day, and doing the hard thing. And they left behind a simple question: Will you?

---

8   Seneca, *Moral Letters to Lucilius*, "Letter VII."

THE BRAVERY EFFECT AND HOW IT'S ALL CONNECTED

Bravery isn't just about mindset. It isn't just about action. And it isn't just about relationships. It's all three—and they are interconnected:

- A brave mindset lays the foundation for action.
  Believing in our ability to grow, reframe fear, and embrace challenges gives us the confidence to step into discomfort and take bold action.

- Brave action strengthens mindset and builds confidence.
  Each time we take action—even when it's uncomfortable—we prove to ourselves that we are capable. This reinforces our

belief in our ability to handle challenges and builds the courage to take on even bigger ones.

- Supportive relationships fuel both mindset and action. Surrounding ourselves with a brave tribe—mentors, friends, and colleagues who encourage and challenge us—reinforces a growth-oriented mindset and provides the accountability and support we need to keep taking action.

Bravery isn't built alone. It's strengthened through a continuous loop where mindset drives action, action builds confidence, and relationships create the support system that keeps us pushing forward. The combined result is the bravery effect. These researchers and thought leaders have shaped my understanding of bravery. Their work proves that bravery is not just a theory; it's a skill that can be developed by anyone willing to do the work.

To the scientists, researchers, and thought leaders who paved the way—thank you. And to the original thinkers, the Stoics, who first recognized the power of courage—your wisdom still holds true today.

STEP INTO BRAVERY

Bravery isn't built in isolation. It's built through action, through practice, through surrounding yourself with the right messages and challenges. If you want to train yourself to be braver, start by immersing yourself in reminders that push you forward.

Take the Bravery Assessment—a simple but powerful tool to measure where you are now and where you can grow. It will help you understand your strengths, pinpoint where fear holds you back, and give you a road map to harnessing the effects of bravery to become the boldest version of yourself.

Follow me on social media and sign up for my newsletter—you'll get regular reminders, insights, and practical strategies to take brave action every single day. I'll challenge you. I'll push you. I'll give you the science-backed tools to stop hesitating and start moving. It won't be easy, but I don't think you'd want it to be. If that sounds too uncomfortable, don't follow me. But if you're ready to be challenged—if you want to build real, lasting courage—let's go. Sign up, take the assessment, and start doing the work.

Bravery isn't something you wait for; it's something you train for. And that training starts now.

JILLSCHULMAN.COM